THE COUNTRY GARDEN

THE COUNTRY GARDEN

JOHN BROOKES

PHOTOGRAPHS BY
JACQUI HURST

CROWN PUBLISHERS, INC. NEW YORK

Senior editor David Lamb
Art editor Meryl Lloyd

Editor Heather Dewhurst

Editorial director Jackie Douglas
Art director Roger Bristow

American editor Marjorie Dietz

Published in the United States by Crown Publishers, Inc.,
225 Park Avenue South, New York, New York 10003 and
represented in Canada by the Canadian MANDA Group.

Published in Great Britain by Dorling Kindersley Publishers
Limited

CROWN is a trademark of Crown Publishers, Inc.

Library of Congress Cataloging-in-Publication Data

Brookes, John, 1933 —
   The country garden.

   Includes index.
   1. Gardening.   2. Landscape gardening.   I. Title.
SB453.B825   1987   712   87-13643
ISBN 0-517-56704-0

Manufactured in Italy

10 9 8 7 6 5 4 3 2 1

First Edition

CONTENTS

THE NEW COUNTRY GARDEN

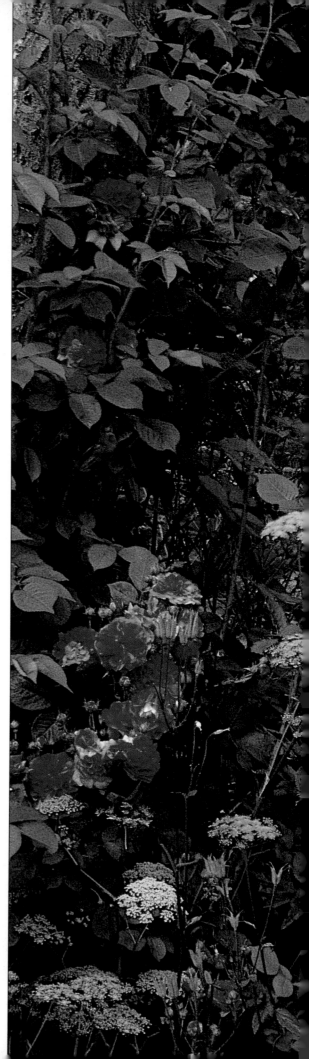

It is undoubtedly true that there is an increasing number of people who seek to live in the country. This desire has been created by all sorts of social situations and conditioning, none more than the decay within many of our inner cities, and the numbing sameness of our vast suburban sprawl. Many are now freed from their city desks by new technologies and can look to the country for a fresh life-style.

But when they do move, what is to stop what was the countryside becoming further surburban sprawl, if not in terms of new building, in the way gardens are gardened? It is high time for a new look at the country garden.

Causes for concern

Many will, in fact, be disappointed with the countryside they move to, holding a romantic image of it in their mind's eye, painted from summer jaunts. The hard fact is that much of the countryside is impoverished. High-output chemical agriculture has led to hedgeless landscapes, inert soils and fewer and fewer farm workers, leaving many villages bereft of young blood. The new country-dweller has to be informed. Country living is more than logs and lambs, it is a way of life conditioned by the all-pervading surroundings, and in most countries those surroundings change very quickly from area to area, depending on the geology and traditional methods of farming. Country-livers must be prepared to become part of the scene and strengthen it, or our countryside will be lost.

The new country look

Plants that no time ago were considered weeds, now have a place in casual-looking mixed plantings. You would include them in a country flower arrangement, why not in a country garden?

Thankfully, there is now a growing concern for the welfare of the countryside, including a concern for the conservation and preservation of native flora and fauna whose habitats are under constant threat. Most new building in the countryside is the result of the same rationing of farm land that leads more and more to unmanageable lots being parcelled off to home owners. Subsequently, new country gardeners often have a plot of illogical dimensions.

They manage their land themselves, between work and a whole range of other recreational activities, and expect to holiday abroad perhaps, leaving the garden once if not twice a year, and so want as many machines as possible to aid them.

Country style gardening

The new country garden is a response to all of these trends. It provides an easy-to-maintain look—a new, essentially country style that can appear random, even unkempt, because beneath the romantic appeal there lies a practical framework.

It is far from being just a summer flower garden. It is one which draws its inspiration from its own location, be it agricultural landscape, rugged moorland, woodland, or any of the many permutations of landscape types. It is a form of gardening that takes a closer look at what grows wild and how it grows, at traditional walls, fences and hedge types, then uses and reflects it to produce a garden that is a visual bonus to its locality.

It is very much the other end of the spectrum to the garden-center, supermarket approach to gardening, which would have our gardens conforming to a universal suburban standard, summed up by all the tackiness that terms such as "patio living" engender. Why should the millions who live and garden in the country (not in stately homes, but in ordinary cottages and houses), and those who want to include country style in their town garden, conform to such a standard with its carrot fly and conifer obsession?

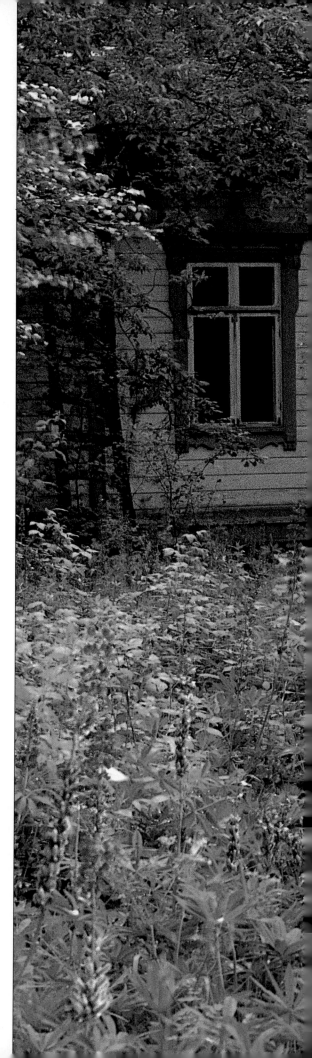

The apartment dweller's dream
Many apartment dwellers have had an alternative country residence for some time. This is a Finnish summer home that provides the perfect magical antidote to city living.

GARDENS IN A LANDSCAPE

The country garden is part of its surroundings in a way its smaller urban counterpart can never be. The country house and its land are not only part of the social community, but they also contribute significantly to the look of the countryside.

Creating and maintaining a country garden encompasses much more than just horticulture and recreation, it is a matter of husbandry—a nice-sounding word, embodying concern. If you have an older property, such concern is for what you have inherited—features such as old trees, ancient walls, and streams or ditches that you care for within your boundaries, but which are part of a much larger network. And concern not only for the structure and plants of your garden, but also for the wide variety of wildlife it attracts.

There is in the country much more of an awareness of before and after, a strong sense of how very transitory we are, scratching away at the few surface inches that we husband during our spell. Instant town gardens can be great fun, but country gardens deserve a long commitment so they can mature like good wine.

TRADITIONAL HUSBANDRY

There will be a traditional form of husbandry, tried and tested by time, ideally suited to the location of your country garden. It will be tempered by your soil and its underlying rock, along with the weather and altitude. To deny traditional husbandry is costly, foolhardy and will keep you ignorant of the spirit of your garden's place, its *genius loci*—the feel of the surrounding landscape that you must come to understand fully if you are to make a really successful country garden.

Your garden as part of the landscape *The scale, planting and "feel" of a surrounding landscape must influence the mood of the garden. How futile to try to improve on the ambience of a location such as the English valley shown left, or to make a decorative show of flowers around the bean and pea-sticks in the garden, right.*

HISTORICAL REVIEW

There have been various schools of thought on the place of a garden within its landscape and their subsequent inter-relationship. The earliest gardens were retreats from the "awe" fulness of nature, for it was overwhelming to a tiny rural commmunity. Its wildness was excluded by high walls or hedges, and within the enclosure our forefathers created their ordered, formal layouts, clipped and neat, as a statement of their superiority and control over nature's seeming disorder. Geometric patterns alone seemed to amuse, with little horticultural content.

Seventeenth-century enclosed garden *The small, enclosed garden of the seventeenth century consisted of box-edged beds containing a limited palette of decorative garden plants arranged in a geometric pattern. Such a formal garden would have been based on similar designs developed in Holland, France and Italy and set out to show man's control over nature.*

This formal tradition extended its limits, and there were permutations of the idea of the enclosed garden through-out sixteenth- and seventeenth-century Europe. The most extensive garden patterns eventually escaped their enclosing walls, and the lines of the geometric layouts were extended into surrounding forest, by out-rides on the Continent and by planted avenues of trees in England where, by the seventeenth century, indigenous forest had been severely denuded for the building of ships and houses. To be successful visually, however, extensive avenues require flat ground, and from the etchings available of the larger formal layouts in England, the young plantings looked bizarre progressing uphill and down dale.

IDEALIZED LANDSCAPE GARDENS
Towards the end of the seventeenth century in England, with the influences of Italian landscape painting and highly

romanticized ideas about the life of the noble peasant, there began to be an appreciation of natural landscape. The interest was fuelled by literature and a concern for Palladian architecture, which, fashion dictated, should be surrounded by parkland in the new "improved" landscape style. The pastoral landscape was allowed to flow to the very walls of the houses so that the views from the mansion, sitting proud and four-square within its domain, were into a controlled landscape, furnished with incidents of Classical origin. Streams were damned to become lakes that reflected this idealized pastoral image and views were molded by mass planting of indigenous trees. The idea of using decorative, exotic plants, and of the decorative garden, was still to be realized but towards the end of the eighteenth century, foreign plant material began to find its way back from the furthest edges of the British empire.

COTTAGE GARDEN TRADITION

There was still a very strict social order pertaining to country life, with the great landlord or squire being the employer, and the remainder of society in his employ, except for the vicar, doctor and school teacher, who stood somewhere on the sidelines. The "big house" garden dominated, and if it was grand enough might have survived to be included on today's round of stately garden tours. But this is not to say that there were no more humble gardens. There was a continuing smaller or cottage garden tradition, which had probably not changed very much since medieval times, in which plants (many of them herbal), were grown for decorative, culinary and medicinal purposes, along with vegetables that were grown solely for domestic use. The planning was haphazard and there was certainly no room for lawns.

The landscape garden *The rolling 'improved' landscape of the eighteenth-century parkland garden was the antithesis of the introspective, protected seventeenth-century garden. Armies of manual laborers were required to subtly remold slopes, shape lakes, plant out groups of indigenous trees and punctuate the whole with decorative Classical incidents, such as temples and statuary.*

The nineteenth century saw enormous social changes and with it the emergence of a new middle class, whose villa homes and smaller gardens created the earliest suburbs. Emphasis was placed on education, particularly concerning things scientific, including botany. Plant exploration became *de rigueur* and the botanic garden was required to show off the latest finds. A whole new horticultural spectrum was on offer, and the nineteenth-century plantsman turned his back on the countryside, put up the barriers again and within them grew the newly-introduced exotic species — plants which in their maturity were bound to make the Victorian garden appear alien to its surroundings. Brilliant color was introduced in geometrically planned beds of annuals and conifers. Rhododendrons and camellias were imported and planted at random (often within the landscape park of the previous century) to create a look that is now considered altogether native in many parts of England.

The Victorian garden *The typical Victorian look was in a style known as "gardenesque". Exotic trees such as the monkey puzzle (Araucaria araucana) were mixed with spectacularly colorful and intricate arrangements of carpet bedding. The conservatory was the home of a further collection of exotics that were too tender for the winter frosts of the outdoor climate.*

TWENTIETH-CENTURY REACTION
At the beginning of the twentieth century there was a reaction to the blatant artificiality of the nineteenth-century look. In Victorian England millions had moved

from the country to the town and as a result, rural life and the countryside were idealized in intellectual circles, giving rise to the Arts and Crafts movement, which pioneered a return to traditional skills and materials. The early twentieth-century garden, therefore, whilst including features of Classical, formal layout, was styled with a feeling for nature, using shrub and perennial plant material that was more suited to its surroundings and more suited to the smaller garden. The feel of the garden, however, was rustic but medieval—it was enclosed, with a layout that had very little to do with the surrounding countryside. Among this last group of gardens are Sissinghurst, in Kent, and Hidcote Manor in Gloucestershire—English models for the country garden worldwide, but made at a time when labor and land were cheap.

Along with a genuine concern for the environment, the economics of the second part of the twentieth century has conditioned the country gardener to reconsider his smaller plot more as part of the landscape in which it sits. The new country garden is allowed to flow through its boundaries, is managed with an eye on tradition but using machinery as an aid, and, furthermore, it fulfills the practical requirements imposed by its users.

The early twentieth-century garden *By the turn of the twentieth century, country garden styling became more rural in fact, although still medieval in its fondness for the garden as a closed room. Planting was full and flowery, and there was a strong sense of tradition through the hard materials used for walls, paving, gates and doors, which were all finished to an exacting level of craftsmanship.*

UNDERSTANDING THE LANDSCAPE

The look of any landscape depends on its underlying geology: substrata of gravel, clay or rock, condition both the texture and the mineral content of the surface topsoil and hence its alkalinity or acidity. The nature of the topsoil in turn supports a natural vegetation that has allowed a certain type of agriculture or forestry to develop. In its turn, traditional local building, to house the people working on the land, was made using available materials—stone or brick, flint or wood—so that regional differences were very apparent.

Conservation is not only concerned with the preservation of the native flora and fauna of a pastoral region, it is also the preservation of its unique character. And it is into this regional tapestry that we insert the country garden.

As gardeners we should be interested in the way these same materials were used for walling and fencing. The local pavings are also relevant, and although one might not copy local style blindly, one might re-interpret it to suit particular requirements.

Similarly, in the selection of plant material, I am not proposing totally "wild" gardening to the exclusion of all else, but on the boundaries of your garden at least you will see how a knowledge of "wild" management is useful, and how native plant material is much easier to cultivate.

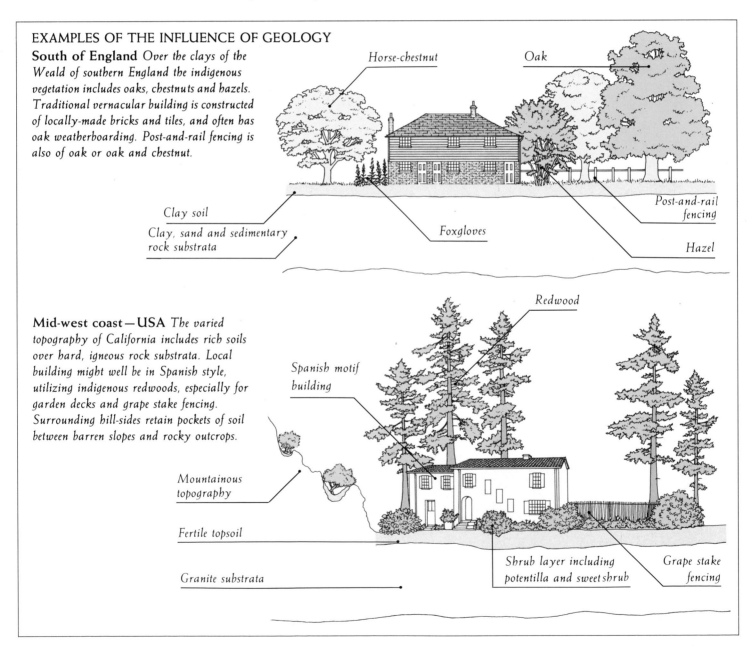

EXAMPLES OF THE INFLUENCE OF GEOLOGY

South of England *Over the clays of the Weald of southern England the indigenous vegetation includes oaks, chestnuts and hazels. Traditional vernacular building is constructed of locally-made bricks and tiles, and often has oak weatherboarding. Post-and-rail fencing is also of oak or oak and chestnut.*

Horse-chestnut

Oak

Clay soil

Clay, sand and sedimentary rock substrata

Foxgloves

Post-and-rail fencing

Hazel

Mid-west coast—USA *The varied topography of California includes rich soils over hard, igneous rock substrata. Local building might well be in Spanish style, utilizing indigenous redwoods, especially for garden decks and grape stake fencing. Surrounding hill-sides retain pockets of soil between barren slopes and rocky outcrops.*

Redwood

Spanish motif building

Mountainous topography

Fertile topsoil

Granite substrata

Shrub layer including potentilla and sweet shrub

Grape stake fencing

BORROWED LANDSCAPE

That your garden can be so much a part of its surroundings is surely a great advantage. Not only will any borrowed scenery beyond your boundary enlarge the apparent size of your plot, it should also serve as inspiration for your garden style, and help in the choice of materials both hard and soft.

The qualities and presence of some landscapes are so strong that they cannot be denied in gardens located within them. The character of such a landscape might be to do with its ground conformation or the extreme quality of a specific soil, which produces a particular vegetation; the presence of woodland, or the immense visual strength of a local material like stone or slate. Any of these strong natural characteristics has to be "used" within the concept of the garden, as imported, substitute forms will seem trivial and out of place.

But not all rural settings have an imposing strength; indeed most have quieter charms that can be just as worthwhile as the dominating landscape, and should similarly be used within your boundaries.

The quiet charms of an agricultural landscape *The gentle slopes of the Downs roll into this Sussex garden in southern England, with their swelling forms repeated in the foreground brick steps.*

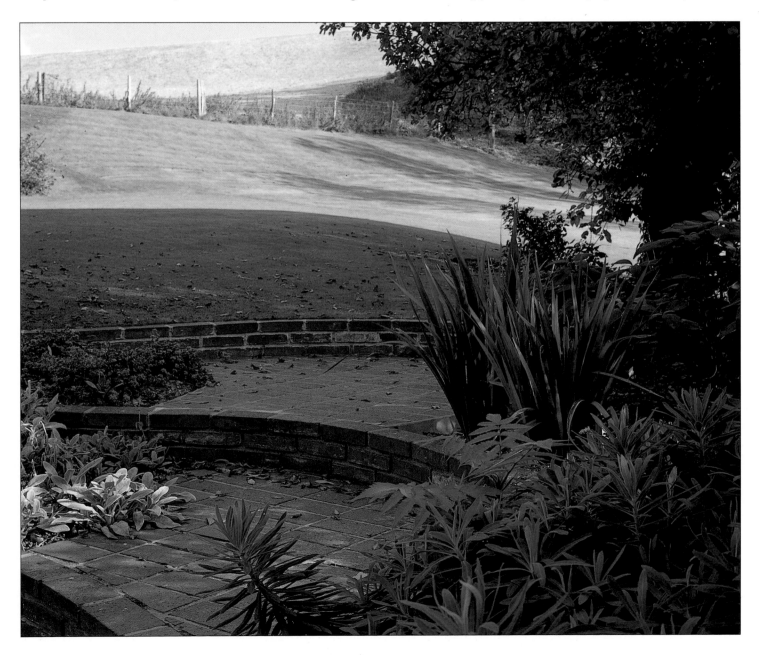

VIEWS OUT

Since it is the natural landscape itself that entices most people to the countryside and encourages them to make their homes there, making the most of any view your country garden may have should be one of your first considerations when creating a new layout, or giving a face-lift to an older one.

But there is more to the job than simply removing a solid barrier for there are two further facts to consider. One is the prevailing weather direction (often the reason that the barrier was erected in the first place), and the other is the scale of the view compared with the scale of your garden. A small, "tamed" plot of land (your garden) set side-by-side with impressive-looking countryside, without a controlled transition between the two can result in the garden looking very insignificant indeed.

A panoramic view can be too much for the eye to encompass, and too expansive for day-to-day appreciation. There are ways to manipulate a view, whilst achieving the right balance between in and out, and at the same time providing weather protection. Seeing just a portion of a fine view, framed by vegetation, makes the transition from a wild landscape to a tamed one more digestible.

CONSIDERING A FRAME

Any framing of a view with vegetation or structure need not necessarily be on or close to the boundary of your garden, where it will emphasize its limits. Framing with planting nearer the viewpoint gives you greater control of the way you see the view, as illustrated in the diagrams opposite. It will also help you to avoid the common fault of evolving a garden design pattern that relates to the boundary, which only reinforces the feeling of enclosure. This means, for example, that if your boundary happens to be L-shaped, it is a mistake to base your garden layout on a series of concentric L-shapes that converge on your house, adjoining it at awkward angles. It is much better to relate your pattern and planting to the house — since it is from this point that you use the garden most, not only physically, but visually as well.

BALANCING SCALE

Controlling a view is also the way to regulate the change from the scale of the garden to the scale of the landscape beyond. There is a balance to be achieved. Framing and reducing the view will prevent what we make of the garden from appearing too trivial when seen against the broad sweep of either a natural or an agricultural landscape.

It will help to remember to keep any formal elements, symmetrical or asymmetrical (walling, paving, hedging and the like), in close proximity to the house or outbuildings, and repeating their lines. There is certainly no place for formal elements near the boundary, if you are trying to open up to a view, since the garden lines, shaping and planting should be as sympathetic to the landscape as possible, to strengthen the transition from in to out.

The space between the area close to the house and the boundary area is best treated in a loose manner, and the styling of its planting planned to progress from the more sophisticated or exotic near the structure (where it will be more sheltered), towards a wilder look the closer it gets to the landscape beyond (see also page 28).

Two-stage view (right) *In this Devonshire garden, planting frames the pasture immediately beyond the garden boundary, as well as a magnificent moorland view beyond that.*

Visual link (below) *The harmonious charm of this garden boundary depends on linear forms of lush garden planting echoing the horizontal lines of hedging and field shapes in the countryside.*

SHAPING A VIEW

To open up a panorama totally is, in most cases, too demanding visually and makes the site too exposed physically. Planting and structures in the garden can be used to shape the view, while at the same time giving protection. Secondary areas of interest can be created within the planting formations, near the viewpoint.

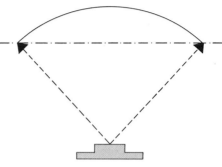

Exposed with a panoramic view

View held and masked

Serpentine planting to restrict the view

View formalized with symmetrical planting

INTEGRATING A VIEW

To integrate a view into a garden layout your general aim is to camouflage the actual boundary line, and to allow the feel of the countryside to run into your property.

Just making a hole in an existing hedge is not always the solution, for what remains of the hedge is still obviously the boundary. You need to plan planting inside the perimeter to bring the view through the hole that has been created, and to strengthen the visual link by counter-balancing any feature outside, with a feature inside.

You will have seen on page 19 how, if there is no existing solid barrier to mark a boundary, an effective way to integrate the view is to plan hedging, or the like, closer to

Making the garden visually stronger
Adding a second tree to the existing willow-leaf pear has the effect of strengthening the garden side of the garden/landscape equation. The view out is now divided by the tree grouping, and foreground garden planting is much reduced compared with the original.

Frame on the garden boundary *Clipped hedges, planted on the garden perimeter, have been shaped to have the effect of framing and holding the view. The position and shape of the hedging gives visual weight to the pear tree, making it an effective counterpoint to the restricted vista beyond.*

the viewpoint. You can then go on to align the piece of your own garden beyond it with the outside world, possibly treating it in a "natural" way with orchard, rough grass and wild flowers.

There are many permutations of this technique — but it is important to be clear in your own mind of the ultimate intention. Then it is important to plan or shape that intention, and finally to style it — that is, to give it the look and feel you think appropriate to your site (see also p.26).

Take another look at the larger photograph on pages 18 and 19, and then at the illustrations below. Each illustration shows an option for a different boundary treatment based on the inviting view shown in the photograph. Each version has a different intention, plan and styling. Those uninitiated in any form of garden design tend to turn the order of basic priorities round the wrong way, thinking first of styling, then plan, which with luck they hope will combine to produce an intention.

Bringing the landscape into the garden *The horizontal flow of the landscape, defined by its hedges, comes sweeping into the garden in this treatment that includes the planting of a foreground willow-leaf pear tree to counterbalance the existing one. Solid lawn planting on either side holds the view.*

The pear tree as a sculptural feature
With the clipped hedge frame close to the viewpoint, the pear tree becomes more of a sculptural feature sitting in the agricultural landscape. The trunk-encircling seat emphasizes the effect by strengthening the visual weight of the tree.

AXES AND VISTAS

Between the enclosed garden of the sixteenth and seventeenth centuries, and the eighteenth century landscape park, there was a transitional period of larger formal layouts, based on dominating axial pathways cut straight across the layout. These axes were often terminated by a dramatic vista of the countryside beyond.

In the nineteenth century, as ranges of alien plant material became available from foreign sources, it was fashionable to create a series of outside garden rooms enclosed by hedges, in which specific plant ranges could be grown. The planning of these outside rooms was again formal and often axial, with controlled vistas created by high planting. This is the tradition followed in the old country gardens at Hidcote Manor in Gloucestershire and Sissinghurst Castle in Kent.

The formal axial tradition can create spectacular linear vistas out of the site—much of their attraction is the contrast between the clipped garden look and the free form of the wild or agricultural landscape beyond. While the vista can be grand and formal, the linear concept can also be re-interpreted more humbly in the manner of a straight path leading to a gate. The way it is paved, and then planted, styles the concept.

Pleached nut arch (right) *Although the styling of this inviting pathway is informal and rustic, the transition from garden to field is formal and axial. The contrast makes a very happy association.*

Informal grandeur (below) *There is an ancient, random quality to this formal build-up of levels to a gateway through the garden wall. The axial planning is reinforced by balanced planting on either side.*

GLIMPSED VIEWS

If your country garden is not blessed with notable panoramas (and this is the case for most of us), if a barn blocks your view from the house to farmland beyond, or if a public right of way ruins your best outlook, all is far from lost. There are invariably ways of using just a glimpse of the countryside to add significantly to the appeal of a part of your garden.

Such a glimpse might be through a distant gateway, between the trunks of trees or over the tops of shrubby plantings. They are delightful bonuses to encounter while strolling. To this end, the route of the path leading to the glimpse is important and might introduce an element of surprise if the approach ensures that the glimpse is revealed at the last possible moment. Those using the path might be encouraged to slow down where they will notice the view ahead by the judicious siting of an inviting seat, or the landing to a generous flight of steps.

A gap between walls (right) *A planting of daisies* (Chrysanthemum maximum) *here masks a simple stile in a fenced gap between flint walls. The gap affords a tempting peek at light woodland beyond.*

A glimpse through planting (below) *A limited view of the countryside beyond foreground planting can be a bonus. This garden's boundary is beneath the far oak, but rough grass brings in the country feel.*

COUNTRY STYLING

So far we have considered the idea of a garden in the country being part of its location, how it should have some identity with its surroundings and fitness for place. But the country garden has also to serve its users and must be designed to that end, with pavings and terraces, with steps and storage spaces—all the necessities of the household, but outside. And it has to be practical in terms of both winter and summer use.

The uses to which you put different areas of the garden should reflect the progression from formal near the house, to wild at the boundary, as discussed on pages 18 and 19. The plan will become looser as it reaches the boundary where the garden fuses into its location. Each zone of the garden (see the diagram on p.28) will have defined uses, with the intermediate area (zone B) being largely reserved for recreation and/or decorative planting.

THE ULTIMATE LOOK
It is the way in which the plan for a garden is realized on site in bricks and mortar (or whatever) and then planted, that extends and brings to final fruition the style of the whole layout, creating a composition totally in sympathy with its ambience, both historically and geographically. Styling is all important for the ultimate look of a garden, but it starts with sound thinking about the layout.

STYLING CLOSE TO YOUR HOUSE
The style of the garden plan should not only reflect the location of the garden, but also the period of your house, particularly close to it in zone A (see p.28). Abstracted linear shapes, for example, are not generally

Faded grandeur (right)
The mood of the planting style of this garden is totally relaxed, although the selection of paving, seat and decorative features is grand to suit the backdrop of an ancient brick wall.

Styling for today's garden (left) *An avenue of trees leading to an urn is a classic garden feature, but this inviting example has a scale and relaxed styling to suit the modern garden.*

considered appropriate for the garden surrounding a period building, though they would be suitable for a modern twentieth-century building. Free or natural shapes are correct for the linear patterns of an eighteenth-century park. More formal classic patterns befit a sixteenth- or seventeenth-century layout, and various permutations of these suit the nineteenth.

But is not only the line of a particular plan (the shape of the paths, terraces, lawns *et al*) that befits a garden to its period, it is also the scale and form of the areas the lines define. Provided that these are correct for a period, I believe there is room for a good deal of re-interpretation of period styles to suit twentieth-century living.

SUITABLE CONSTRUCTION DETAILS
We have seen how all the materials of house structure, its walls and fences, and the plants that surrounded it, were once indigenous—their massed effect is a chief ingredient in, for example, the strong characters of a mellow-stoned Gloucestershire hamlet or a limestone dales village. In the latter part of the twentieth century, however, we have a far greater range of materials from which to select, and far easier access to the builder's merchants and garden

centers that supply them. It is a strange contradiction that those local materials we would ideally use are now often too expensive, so that we have to re-think what is suitable within the traditional context.

You will have to study styles of walling and coping, looking closely at the elevations of buildings to discern not only the types of material used but the way in which they were used and the styling of their details.

Even if you have to use new materials, make sure their use complies with traditional methods. This will help to unite your house with the garden near to it.

STYLING AND YOUR BOUNDARY
For the correct styling of your boundary area (zone C on p.28) you will need to turn your back to the house. At one time, the boundary area of a country garden would have been styled with the house and from the same palette of materials and plants. Now you can look to the shape and configuration of fields beyond, and note the prevalent

Planting close to the house *A conscious profusion of plants creates a softening random effect against architectural features. 'Goldheart' ivy, climbing hydrangea and golden hop clothe the walls.*

THE ANATOMY OF A COUNTRY GARDEN
The process of styling your country garden will be considerably assisted by mentally dividing the plot into the three zones shown in this diagram. The approach is intended as a guide, not a set of

rules, since in any particular garden unique qualities will require special treatment. In a small garden, for example, you could use the zone C treatment throughout.

Zone A Area adjacent to building
This is the area reserved for any formal treatment that you may wish to give to your garden. The plan should be conceived to follow the form of the house, and realized in materials sympathetic to the structure. Planting can be bold in form and color, but always in tune with the building.

Zone B Transitional area
In this zone, your style progresses from domestic to landscape in a way that suits the topography, weather and scale of the garden. This is the area that varies in size from garden to garden, depending on the overall size of the garden in question. It is often an area used for recreation with planting to suit, but tempered by the desired progression towards wilder planting as it approaches zone C.

Zone C Boundary area
The aim, in the boundary area, is to develop planting that is in complete sympathy with the countryside beyond so that the boundary line itself goes unnoticed. If you need a physical boundary, then it should be of a sort to match local types so that the effect is unobtrusive.

kinds of boundary, looking for clues. Study local plant formations, including hedge types, note the dominant species of solitary field trees, as well as those in surrounding woods and copses.

Most of us are probably aware of certain classic plant groups—heathers, heaths, birch and Scots pine on an acid soil, for example. There is, in northern Europe at least, a chalky soil association including wild clematis, native box, yew and euonymus (wayfaring tree), and on the Chilterns, in central southern England, one of beech with wild white cherry on the perimeter. On heavy clay soils hedging will be of thorn quicks, and ash and oak are the dominant trees.

Lowering your sights, look for wild plant types, gradually building a picture of the natural plant forms surrounding your garden. A good plant dictionary will point you to associated cultivated forms of the wild plants you have noted.

PLANTING AND STYLING

It is interesting that the different types of country garden planting often appear to be the strongest feature of country style. Everyone thinks of cottage style planting, for example, as the epitome of English country style. In fact, without the underlying structure of the style, the subsequent planting would probably not read nearly so strongly. It is very easy to be tempted to buy plants first, swayed by their immediate appeal, without being sure of the framework in which they will fit.

This is not to say that country gardening is not about plants. As you will see later in this book, some styles of country garden depend on flowers, for example, for their look (see p.108). But the use of plants ought to suit the feel you create, and that feel will be strongest and easiest to maintain if it is inspired by the ambience that your plot undoubtedly has. Design your ideal layout first without being distracted by the details of planting plans. Once you are sure of the overall concept you can progress to choosing the exact content of each planting area.

Profusion by a boundary wall (right) *At one time, the country garden would have been formally controlled to the very foot of grand boundary walls. Lesser means and regard for natural forms now allow a more relaxed approach.*

Twentieth-century styling (below) *The layout and use of elements has a modern feel but blends perfectly with the traditional buildings in this garden. Rampant climbers and gravel planting complete the setting.*

LOOKING FOR INSPIRATION

I can hear the horticulturally-minded reader thinking that the only ambience that many country plots have at the outset is the look of a disused farmyard, and the only way to cope with it is to dig and clip and tidy until it is transformed into an enclosure "fit" for horticultural

Style from existing structures *An outhouse and old carriage yard paved in granite blocks, provide the inspiration for a country garden style of relaxed, muddled charm.*

display. But look at that untidy farmyard again and you might just see the potential of its charm and how it can be the perfect inspiration for your garden styling. That you cannot at first afford to have an old barn or modest farm structure demolished in your first flush of enthusiasm might just turn out to be the best thing you ever did for your garden. It could turn into the element that sets the style for the rest of your garden. Such an element will have the undoubted advantage of looking as though it belongs and might well have a distressed charm that would otherwise take years to develop.

The worse place for inspiration is probably your local garden center. Wandering around there for too long without a specific idea of your requirements is likely to result in an island bed of decorative conifers or heathers that completely belie their location. It is much better to spend your time walking or driving in your locality, soaking up the details of its charm that attract you, and assessing whether or not you might interpret them within your own boundaries. Visiting local craft fairs is also a good idea for they often encourage displays of traditional fieldcrafts that might be useful to you, including dry-stone walling, hurdle making and hedge laying (see p.39). Using such craftsmanship in your plot might re-awaken a spirit of place you never imagined was there.

Styling the country garden then, is not simply a matter of decoration and details, it is also the conception of a plan and working with what you have to fulfil your requirements for country living.

Farmyard style *Some borrowed landscape across a paddock provides the backdrop to thatched outbuildings dripping with roses. This is not a "garden" in the accepted sense, but could it be improved?*

ENTRANCES AND EXITS

The mood of any particular country garden style is initiated by the main entrance, the dimensions of which nowadays are largely dictated by the width of your car. If seen against the house, the same styling as chosen for the house surrounds is appropriate for the entrance, harmonizing with the architectural style of the house. There is a balance to be struck between welcome and privacy when styling entrances, remembering that the most compelling entrances are a combination of structure and planting that tempts one to see what comes next.

Pedestrian entrances are most successful when treated as part of the incidental decoration of the garden and have most charm if their styling is understated and in complete harmony with planting as exemplified by the simple wooden gate opening on to a Berkshire garden, opposite. Next to it grows the large-leaved ivy, *Hedera colchica*.

Stone and brick archway *A heavy-looking archway such as this depends on surrounding planting for its softening effect.*

Classic iron gate *The beauty of a good iron gate is that it provides an effective barrier without impeding the view.*

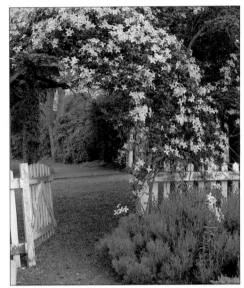

Cottage garden gate *A white picket fence and matching gate is here suitably arched over with spring-flowering* Clematis montana.

Picket gates within an archway *Simple picket gates contrast with the grandeur of this brick-faced archway with iron decoration.*

Field gate *For many country property entrances, variations of the traditional five-bar gate are ideal.*

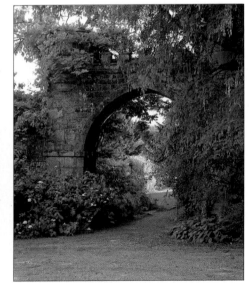

Stone arch *Planting balances the visual weight of this massive stone arch that serves as an inviting entrance to a Yorkshire garden.*

GARDEN WALLS

The walled garden (as part of a larger estate) for the protection of fruit and vegetables, a nursery garden or a pleasance, has medieval origins. The high, brick-built walls of such enclosures still exist and are one of the hallmarks of the traditional English country garden.

In a new plan, the expense of building walls can be prohibitive, but their value for linking buildings visually with elements of the garden, molding space and strengthening character, is invaluable. Every type of wall has its own special charm, ranging from warm and friendly to tough and forbidding and, built in the vernacular style, a wall will forge a strong link between your garden and its surroundings. Every region has its local walling style or styles, based on available materials, whether clay (baked into many different types of brick) or stone. Brick walls are bonded with mortar, the modern version of which remains unaffected by the aerial roots of clinging plants, such as ivy. Dry-stone walling is an art that requires years of practice to perfect but can be learned by the enthusiastic amateur keen to make a good repair.

It is very difficult to justify removing an old wall—they are nearly always an immense asset visually, even in a next-to-ruinous state. No garden element creates privacy in quite the same way, nor provides a better foil to foliage.

Stone and brick *Obviously, one must concede that a new wall would look bland compared with this lichen-rich mixture of dressed stone and bricks, laid without mortar.*

Lime-washed brick *A vine (Vitis sp.) and a simple, pelargonium-planted window-box are the perfect clothing for an old brick house wall, pierced by what was once an internal oven.*

Honey-color stone *Mellowed stonework, such as in this house wall in Worcestershire, glows in the sunshine and complements the stems and blooms of old roses.*

Ancient dry-stone wall *With time, mosses and lichens will establish themselves in dry-stone walls. They have to be constructed of stone that splits in one direction, such as limestone or slate.*

Slate retaining wall *Slabs of slate, laid vertically, make a low retaining wall of sculptural beauty. Such details lend great character to gardens in areas where slate is quarried.*

Old brick *The brick elevations of walled gardens are the traditional support and shelter of fruit-bearing plants, including fruit tree cordons such as these, and espalier-trained specimens.*

Coursed flint work *In areas where chalk occurs naturally, flint walls are in order. This wall is faced with whole, rounded flints— sometimes they are split, or "knapped".*

FENCING AND HEDGING

Whereas walling has its place close to the house, and is ideal as a boundary within which to make a country fantasy in town, it is expensive and can make too definite a visual barrier between inside and out for the country location. Fencing or hedging are more appropriate. If you do need a new fence or hedge, or need to replace one, look to the local traditional types for both the right look and value for money. In many British locations, cleft chestnut or larch rails between oak posts are fairly common.

Some excellent zig-zag, pioneer-type timber stock fences were used in the United States before the advent of barbed wire. They consist of pairs of posts with each pair at 45 degrees to the next pair. The horizontal timbers are slotted between the pairs. Traditional woven sheep hurdles of willow or hazel, bound between stout cleft posts look excellent for five years or so, before they rot. Use them also for sheltering new plantations from the wind.

Timber fences need a wire netting or chain link backup to make them stock- and rabbit-proof. Chain link is more expensive but lasts longer—both are invisible at a distance. Bury the bottom edge of the wire 150 mm (6 in) deep, taking it up to the first horizontal on the post and rail fences and at least halfway up the hurdles.

Low, wrought or cast-iron railings have been used for a more sophisticated rural look since the eighteenth century, particularly in England and Ireland. Painted black, they too have the virtue of becoming totally invisible from a distance, since the horizontals are so thin.

Post-and-rail fencing *One of the beauties of traditional post-and-rail fencing, such as this three-rail example dividing a spring garden from sheep in the field beyond, is that you can see through it.*

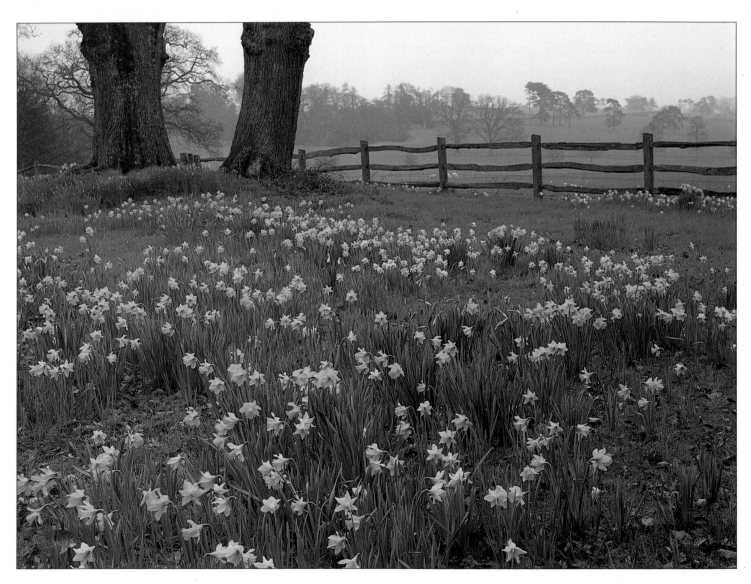

As with timber fencing, wrought-iron railings can also be made rabbit-proof using wire netting.

HEDGING

It is a sad fact that many of the plants used to create a traditional type of hedge are not particularly fast growing, and it is for this reason that one sees so much *Chamaecyparis leylandii* used. But the visual effect of this straggling conifer in maturity has a devastating effect upon the countryside. Of native or naturalized plants, hawthorn (*Crataegus* spp.), blackthorn (*Prunus spinosa*) and field maple (*Acer campestre*) grow fastest though none are evergreen. Holly (*Ilex* spp.) makes an excellent impenetrable evergreen hedge. Gorse (*Ulex europaeus*), *Rosa rugosa* cvs. and beech (*Fagus sylvatica*) can also be used.

Fence and hedge combination *While the embryo hedge on this boundary establishes itself, a softwood post-and-rail fence serves as an attractive temporary division.*

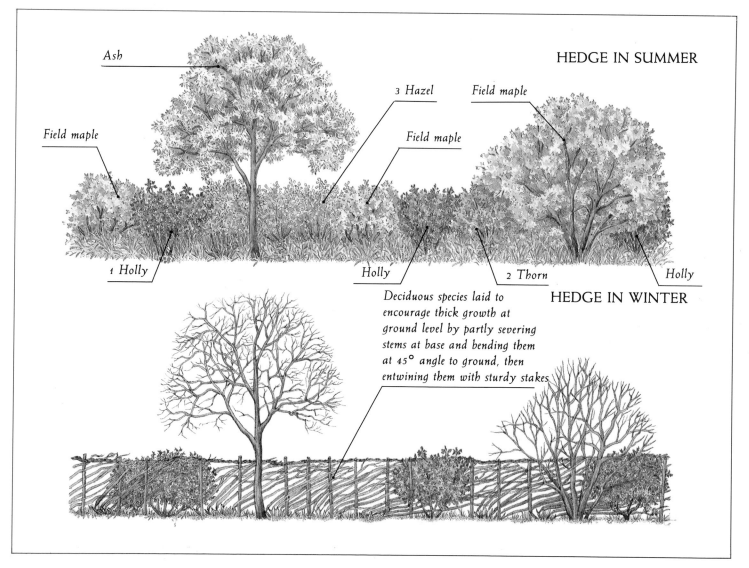

Ash

HEDGE IN SUMMER

3 Hazel

Field maple

Field maple

Field maple

1 Holly

Holly

2 Thorn

Holly

HEDGE IN WINTER

Deciduous species laid to encourage thick growth at ground level by partly severing stems at base and bending them at 45° angle to ground, then entwining them with sturdy stakes

SURFACES AND LEVELS

The areas of a country garden closest to the house are made up of differing levels (comprising paths, terraces, yards and planting) interconnected by steps and/or ramps. When seen on plan, it is the correct proportion of these level areas, linked to the house, that should make a visually satisfying collage effect of interlocking shapes.

CHANGES OF LEVEL

Steps linking changes of level should be regarded more as a feature than a necessity and, if planned generously enough, become a series of landings that encourage leisurely perambulation. The landings lend themselves to decoration with planted pots and provide viewpoints.

Ideally, changes of level, which may well include some type of retaining wall, should be constructed either in the same material, or have some affinity to the surfacings of areas which they connect. Preferably, they should have a proportional relationship as well.

THE PROPORTIONS OF STEPS

The material of which the steps are made will, to a degree, dictate their proportions but, broadly speaking, step treads look well approximately 45 cm (18 ins) deep, with a riser of about 15 cm (6 ins). This allows an average pace as one goes up or down. Consider the function of riser and tread, depending on the dimensions and form of material you have chosen. Bricks on edge and stone make steps with crisp edges that will wear with time. Using some form of slab material makes it possible for the tread to overhang the risers, creating shadow and increasing sculptural form.

The form of the steps should be dictated by the garden layout. Steps designed within traditional, formal layouts tend to be centralized within the plan and comprise one grand flight. But for a more casual effect, steps may be staggered, they may turn on a landing or even have larger areas between the risers.

With the increasing use of heavy machinery to maintain the garden, steps can be a hazard to negotiate, and ramps become a necessary alternative. These are simpler, and therefore cheaper, to construct than steps, but they deserve just as much consideration as to their location and material of construction. If you plan to use a loose material, such as gravel, shingle or wood bark, the gradient of the ramp must be kept to a minimum or its surface will be washed away. A combination of shallow ramps with intermediate landings may be the solution. For heavy wear, consider using granite blocks or engineering bricks set at an angle (haunched) in mortar over hardcore.

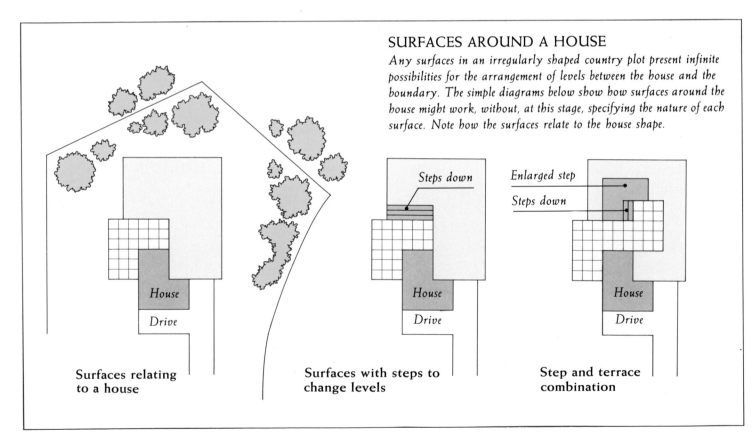

SURFACES AROUND A HOUSE

Any surfaces in an irregularly shaped country plot present infinite possibilities for the arrangement of levels between the house and the boundary. The simple diagrams below show how surfaces around the house might work, without, at this stage, specifying the nature of each surface. Note how the surfaces relate to the house shape.

Surfaces relating to a house

Surfaces with steps to change levels

Step and terrace combination

Steps "au naturel" *In a landscape of rocky outcrops, such as the hard, granite face of Cornwall, what could be more appropriate than steps that resemble natural outcrops, engulfed by natural plant forms, including mosses, ferns and a variety of grasses?*

Worn stone steps *These beautifully simple steps have random stone treads that have become dished with the passing of countless feet. The steps link with a brick terrace punctuated with soil pockets that have allowed plants to self-seed, particularly Alchemilla mollis.*

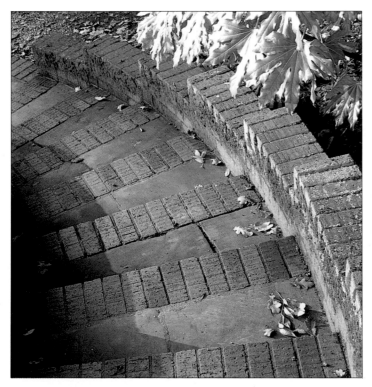

Curved flight *Attention to the details of construction make this curved flight of steps both a useful pathway and an elegant garden feature. The treads are of slabs, with brick edging that links visually and physically with a stepped retaining wall.*

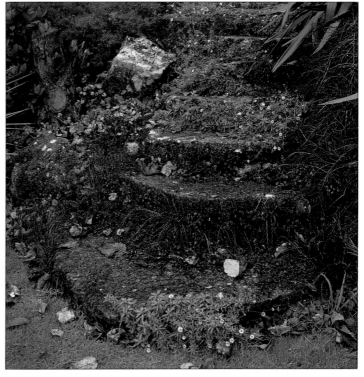

Shaped stone treads *The charm of this substantial flight of shaped stone steps in autumn, lies in the combination of hard material and random planting, including barberry and daisy flowers. The flight as a whole is more of a decorative feature than a useful path.*

CHANGES OF LEVEL

One of the great differences between a country plot and the suburban norm is that country sites are often blessed with natural changes of level between one part of the garden and another. This might just be the gentle rise and fall associated with fertile lowlands, but it might be much more dramatic, including steep slopes and even rock outcrops. I say "blessed with" because many gardeners faced with billiard table flatness go to great lengths to create different levels for interest's sake, while others are unable to justify the upheaval and expense involved unless excavations are anyway required for new building or features such as ponds.

Whether man-made or natural in origin, there are two basic ways of manipulating changes of level to advantage. You either follow natural lines, making sure that any new slope or bank is contoured in a realistic way (see the garden plan on p.57), or you use the artifice of terracing, where flat areas are connected by banks, ramps or flights of steps. The two gardens below are examples of layouts where the whole character of the garden depends on the treatment of changes of level, including steps and terraces.

PRACTICALITIES

It is a very simple job for a surveyor to plot useful spot heights across your site, from a zero point such as your front door step. These points will help you to assess the number of steps of a particular height required to traverse a slope. Otherwise, take a tape and mark meter intervals from top to bottom of the slope. Then measure the vertical height from one point to a straight-edge held level (use a spirit-level) above it and projecting from the next meter mark up the slope. Duplicate the process for each of the meter marks and you can add up the total rise of the measured distance.

When undertaking any land shaping it is vital to ensure that topsoil remains on top. It should be removed and set aside before the subsoil layers are touched so that after molding it can be replaced.

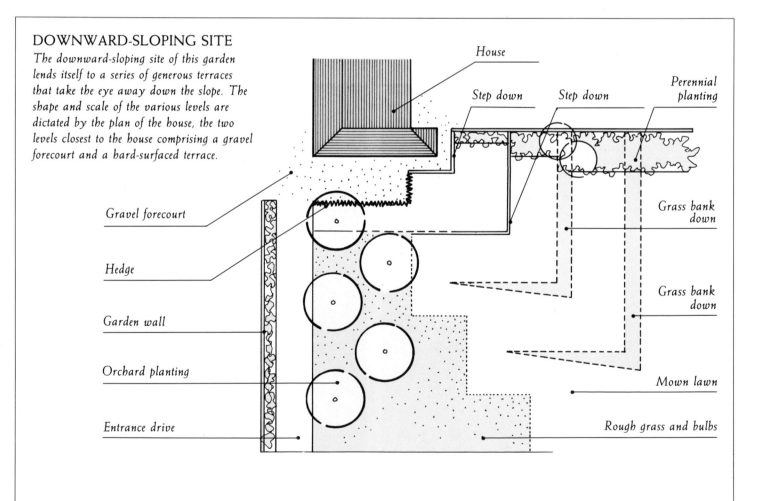

DOWNWARD-SLOPING SITE

The downward-sloping site of this garden lends itself to a series of generous terraces that take the eye away down the slope. The shape and scale of the various levels are dictated by the plan of the house, the two levels closest to the house comprising a gravel forecourt and a hard-surfaced terrace.

House

Step down — Step down

Perennial planting

Gravel forecourt

Hedge

Garden wall

Orchard planting

Entrance drive

Grass bank down

Grass bank down

Mown lawn

Rough grass and bulbs

The most common fault when planning changes of level is failing to achieve a balance of scale between the areas of the levels. Close to the house, terraces ought to relate to the area and shape of the house plan and should be generous enough to make a visual balance with it. Often they are too small and can never look anything but niggardly and out of proportion.

Interconnecting terraces often make for layouts of great interest and dynamism, leading the eye to the top or bottom of the terraced levels and towards views or prime features within the site. As with all garden design, get the pattern and shape of your layout right first, then worry about surfacing materials.

Any main pathway or year-round sitting area, particularly where there are steps, requires some form of hard surfacing in sympathy with the location. Otherwise the surfaces to choose from include turf (including rough grass as opposed to mown grass), groundcover plants, such as hypericum and spurge, cobbles and even larger fragments of rock. As a finishing touch there are a wide range of pots and other decorative features that can be positioned at various points to punctuate your plan.

UPWARD-SLOPING SITE

In this example, the house (with an adjacent barn) nestles beneath a rock face. The layout makes dramatic use of the upward-sloping site, including a grand flight of steps up to the highest point of the garden, and retaining walls shaped to match the dynamic plan.

Existing lime tree (Tilia *sp.*)

Retaining wall

Planted pots

Shale bank

Rock fragments

Rock face

2 Hazels (Corylus avellana)

House

Shade groundcover planting

Barn

PAVINGS

There are many diverse surface materials suitable for the pavings of a country garden, though physical criteria often make their selection impractical. Some surfacings, for instance, become slippery in winter; others pick up on damp boots and get carried indoors. Overriding these considerations, however, should be the visual fitness of the materials you choose for their context. Local stone, local gravel or local brick will never look inappropriate, and since it will not cost as much to transport them to you, they should be comparatively cheap. However, the major expense of paving is the cost of labor and, broadly speaking, the smaller the individual paving element the more expensive it will be to lay.

MIXING PAVINGS

Pavers, slightly larger than standard brick size, are being used more and more, but too much of this surfacing, like too much of any one surfacing, can appear too urban and slick for the country setting. Stone, on the other hand, is becoming more and more difficult to obtain. But what about mixing the materials to create a random, textured feel? Granite blocks can be used in the mixture in granite areas, as can cobbles where they are available.

Pre-cast concrete paving slabs can be useful. Muted colors are better, but the chances are that a local firm making them will use the local stone as aggregate so their color will blend with any existing structure. I prefer to use a textured slab whose pattern does not simulate stone.

JOINTING

The way in which jointing is completed makes an enormous difference to paving. It can be flush with the surface or given a trowelled slant, but neither technique looks as good as the joint being "rubbed back" slightly, that is, before the mortar of the joint sets hard, it is scraped away to just below the surface of the paving. The color of the mortar joint should also be considered and altered if necessary (by choice of sand color or by color additive).

Planting in paving *Expanses of one type of paving will tend to look too urban in the country garden. A satisfying mix of paving types to adjoin a low stone wall can be made by combining random-sized, natural stone slabs with granite blocks. The visual toughness of the stone is balanced by a planting of euphorbias and ivy.*

All the paving is laid on a consolidated base, but if you backfill the joints between the elements with topsoil, grass and self-seeders such as alchemilla will soften the look.

Euphorbia wulfenii

Ivy

Alchemilla mollis

Textured pre-cast slab *Pre-cast concrete paving slabs provide a sound, not-too-expensive surfacing material.*

Random flints *This is a traditional paving type that looks marvellous with flint-faced buildings, but is time-consuming to lay.*

Stable tiles *These squares come in blocks of six, and were originally used in stables. They make a pleasant, small-scale pattern.*

Random stone paving *Laying random stone as well as this takes skill and time to ensure satisfying interlocking shapes.*

Distressed brick and stone *The charm of much country paving results from growth between the elements, such as this green moss.*

Brick and stone combination *A mixture of large and small paving elements can be very attractive, but requires careful planning.*

York stone slabs *Natural stone slabs produce a handsome, massively-scaled floor pattern. Plants will self-seed in the joints.*

Brick pavers *Specially hard, brick-sized pavers, or house bricks if they are sufficiently hard-baked, can be laid in many patterns.*

Simulated granite blocks *Pre-cast concrete slabs that simulate granite blocks can be remarkably attractive if well laid.*

GARDEN WALKS

Could you resist the allure of the walk shown opposite? Its shady, overgrown character seems irresistible and epitomizes the charm of the best garden walks, those that tempt you to explore, to see what is round the corner or at the end of the vista. It is the abundance of greenery on either side of a walk that gives it its particular allure while other features can be an added bonus. The large mossy rock beside the walk opposite appears to be strategically placed to encourage the passer-by to stop, sit and wonder at the beauty of the surroundings. Such a path is not a main route through the garden, it is an incident within the total, styled to suit its particular site.

Between buildings *A garden walk between buildings can be very tempting. Here the distant viewpoint is a strong attraction, as is the expectation of views around corners.*

Towards woodland *A planting of astilbe lines one side of this gravelled garden walk that disappears into woodland. Rubus tricolor provides groundcover on the left.*

Behind a building *A pollarded tree trunk and an old cask used as a water butt furnish this concrete-surfaced walk that disappears behind an old timber-faced building.*

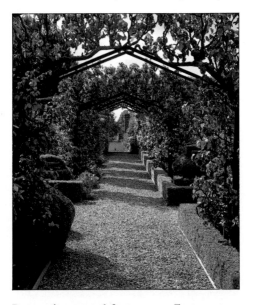

Between clipped box *This gravel walk edged with stone tiles, in a New England-type garden, has a formal charm. Box-edged beds filled with herbs, demand closer attention.*

Through abundant planting *Old roses, alchemilla and a globe artichoke with handsome gray leaves line a romantic gravel path that leads to a flower garden.*

Beneath trained fruit trees *Fruit trees trained over frames force the view down this path. The style is architectural suggesting a complex network of paths to explore.*

GARDEN BUILDINGS

If your house has not set the style of your country garden, its outbuildings may; for one of the great virtues of older houses in the country is that they are often accompanied by a barn, or an old coach house, a bothy, a shed or even a pigsty. All can be used as features in a layout, while the form of such a structure will give clues to the sort of materials you might use elsewhere in the garden. Defunct farm shelters are sometimes a bonus as they might provide a sheltered courtyard that can be gravelled.

Always consider a change of use for a structure that might at first seem outmoded, especially if it was originally

Converted stabling *Old brick and tile loose boxes have been skilfully worked into the layout of this garden, for use as storage units. Planting and tubs turn the structure into a handsome addition to the garden.*

built in the same style as the house and on a suitable scale. Nothing would be more inappropriate, for example, than to remove a traditional shelter, and then to turn to a catalogue of pre-fabricated garages, when, with a little thought, the original would have served your car admirably and have blended perfectly visually.

It is very easy to be tempted by advertisements offering "period" conservatories and other garden buildings. Although some of these offer a credible match to some styles of building, if available in the right scale, many are over-ornamented with decorative details that are a parody of the original model. The country home and garden deserve much simpler, more practical structures.

Some modern outbuildings now have considerable character. Not the garden-center cedar wood shed, which is still far too "thin" and lacking in substance for a country garden feature, but new timber stabling and loose boxes or dog runs, which can look well-proportioned, stocky and practical, despite their newness.

One of the problems of siting and using small buildings within a layout is their scale—their ground plan is often too small for their height, and they easily become a pimple on the plot. Where they are absolutely necessary, it is a good idea to attach such a building to another structure to bulk up the overall feel.

DECORATIVE QUALITIES VERSUS PRACTICALITY

The type of building that you have in a garden might be either decorative or practical; if the latter, your planting can improve it. It pays to remember, however, that the purely decorative eye-catching building quickly becomes a liability, since its maintenance is so high. Unless extremely well built, deterioration of such buildings soon sets in due to their lying unused for long periods, especially through winter dampness. Furthermore, such a building can all too easily become a secondary store, a glory hole for mowers, redundant garden furniture, or last summer's barbecue. Such usage will soon remove any decorative qualities that the building had.

The more practical garden building can be designed or converted to provide specific storage areas, including tool sheds and such like, to meet the increasing demand for adequate, secure storage in country gardens. The charm of such buildings will lie in their functional structure, how comfortably they fit into the garden layout, the paved approach to them and their complementary associated planting, as you will see on page 51.

Focal point of a garden *A splendid tower was designed as the focal point of this stylish garden. It provides a usable store at ground level and studio/office space with a fine view, above.*

BUILDINGS AND PLANTS

One of the joys of the natural-looking garden is the way rampant but controlled plant growth modifies the look of buildings. A structure can be transformed by the softening influence of plants that will clothe walls. They might grow up against it (like ceanothus), grow on supports fixed to the wall (either twining like jasmine or tied in like a rambling rose), or cling by means of aerial roots (like ivy).

Although ivies and evergreen honeysuckle are indispensable for their year-round contribution, most dramatic in their seasoned visual impact on a building are deciduous climbers that grow up quickly through spring and summer. The hop, for example (*Humulus lupulus*), will scramble up and over a building and bear attractive fruit clusters at an astonishing rate, before dying back as winter approaches. Prior to planting, construct a substantial network of wires against the wall to support the climber.

CONSERVATORIES

The classic meeting of building and plants, however, is in the conservatory, or glasshouse. There has been a revival of interest in the conservatory recently, fired by the manufacture of glazed units designed to provide both a home-extension and a place in which to grow plants.

The "clothed" building *A deciduous climber, such as this hop, will transform a building during its growing season. As such a plant dies back, make sure you remove all old growth from roof tiles, gutters and other important structural elements of a building.*

These two functions are difficult to combine, however, for conservatory plants need copious amounts of water, including spraying—requirements that do not mix with indoor furnishings. A small glazed extension can suffer from extreme fluctuations of temperature. Sited to catch the sun's rays, it will become too hot for plants in mid-summer and may become surprisingly cold at night.

Traditionally, the conservatory is a larger building, kept separate from the general living area. It might indeed be free-standing, a stroll away from the garden doors of the house. It is a place in which to brighten the dull days of late winter (for those of us in the chillier temperate zones) and to enjoy the fragrance and color of tender, or out-of-season blooms. Its size makes fluctuations of temperature less extreme and easier to control.

Building a new conservatory along traditional lines involves major expense, but you might be lucky enough to inherit one that will respond to a little judicious renovation. Then you will have to decide whether to heat it or not, remembering that to warm a single-glazed house to even modest temperatures is an expensive business. Without heat, it is still possible to bring on early spring and summer flowers with great success.

PAVILIONS

If you free yourself from the task of keeping an exotic plant collection, your requirements for a garden building are less exacting and you might settle for a structure with large glazed areas in the elevations (so that you can use it partly as a greenhouse), but with a traditional roof of tiles, slates or shingles. Such a structure might be called a pavilion (for want of a better term) and will be most successful if it can fulfil a practical function, providing shelter or shade near a terrace, for example.

PAVILION ADJOINING TERRACES

This is a construction idea for a pavilion that links two terraces bounded by an existing high brick wall. The pavilion is hexagonal with brick elevations to match the walling, pierced by large windows and a matching double door for access. The pitched roof is tiled. The stone flags used to surface the two terraces also make up the treads of two steps that follow the line of the building. It is important that surrounding planting is full and allowed to flop on to the paving, softening the overall look of the building and the hard surfacing.

Tiled roof

Glazed doorway

Full mixed planting

Random York stone flags

Steps up

Sawn York stone paving

Bricks to match existing garden wall

THE GARDEN IN WINTER

I think every winter is more beautiful than the last. From a gardener's point of view there is satisfaction in the "put to bed" look of early winter—with leaves finally raked, debris removed and farmyard manure spread. Shapes are strong in the garden at this time of the year too—shapes of lawns and shapes of paths, and the strong shapes of evergreens that come into their own as their deciduous neighbors are reduced to skeletons. I love the black look of yew (*Taxus* sp.), and, if the winter is mild, the green of early hellebores with the pale yellow of winter jasmine seen against them.

The pleasures of a winter garden are generally subtle however—no banks of color here, but what pleasure from the earliest snowdrops and aconites, and the first waves of scent from the winter honeysuckle (*Lonicera fragrantissima*), sarcococca and hamamelis. Sharp frosty mornings invigorate, and there is always a clear conscience about garden chores. It is time for a country walk to soak in the neat black and white look that stretches out from your garden to the landscape beyond, for at no time of year does the garden blend better with its backdrop. Now is the time to study the natural contours that surround your garden. Sloping ground beyond your boundaries will establish a rhythm where the ridges of slopes intersect—a rhythm that you might interpret in the pattern of your layout.

After snow there's a further magic. The small detail is hidden and only large, broad shapes register. If the proportions of your garden look good in mid-winter, with shrub masses working in scale with their backdrop, then your garden will only improve during the luxuriant, growing months of spring and summer.

Delights (right) *Late winter's compensations include the blooms of giant snowdrops (*Galanthus elwesii*) and Helleborus corsicus, with the marbled leaves of Arum italicum 'Marmoratum'.*

Garden in a winter landscape (left) *Evergreen shapes show up well in the stark winter landscape, in this case yew (*Taxus baccata*), and monkey puzzles (*Araucaria araucana*).*

WINTER FLOWERS

There is a quiet, delicate beauty to winter's flowers. They are
usually of pale colors, particularly soft greens, and many are highly
scented. This array was cut from my garden in southern England in
December, after an unusually mild start to winter. Winter blooms
do not form flamboyant displays but are gems to discover when
much of the garden lies dormant and strong foliage
shapes are center stage.

Cyclamen *A hardy variety, the
brave blooms of which have a
delicious fragrance*

**Cupressus arizonica
'Conica'** *Produces a sea
of tiny yellow flowers*

Viburnum fragrans *A deciduous
viburnum but produces scented
florets well into winter*

Viburnum tinus (left)
*Evergreen, with eye-catching
florets throughout winter*

**Rosemary (Rosmarinus officinalis
'Fastigiatus')** *Light frosts allow
rosemary flowers to survive*

**Autumn-flowering
cherry (Prunus
subhirtella
'Autumnalis')**

Ivy (Hedera helix) *Ivy flowers
are often ignored but have a
graphic quality*

**Winter jasmine
(Jasminium
nudiflorum)** *Flowers
unfailingly on bare stems*

Euphorbia wulfenii
*Tenacious, green flowerheads are
a winter-time bonus*

Mahonia japonica *The scented racemes
of this shrub complement its striking leaf shape*

Stinking hellebore (Helleborus foetidus) *Large green flowers with strongly-shaped foliage*

Iris foetidissima *The brilliant fruit of this iris has all the visual appeal of its summer flowers*

Christmas rose (Helleborus niger) *Has flowers of a paper-like, ephemeral quality*

Helleborus corsicus *Delicate, apple-green blooms amongst leathery, serrated-edged leaves*

Silk tassel bush (Garrya eliptica) *Produces pendulous, showy catkins at their best in mid winter*

Primula *A ubiquitous, but always pleasing wintertime to early spring flower, best in wild primrose-like lemons*

Sweet box (Sarcococca hookeram) *Tiny buds herald masses of fragrant, pale-yellow flowers*

Daphne odora *Evergreen with fragrant flowers that typify winter's gem-like blooms*

Ivy (Hedera colchica 'Paddy's Pride') *Produces characteristic pompon flower clusters*

REPLANNING

Winter is an ideal time for replanning, when you can see the line and pattern of your garden most sharply while it rests stark and clear from the blur of vegetation. It is also pleasant to be creative in those dead days of the season when there are no pressing garden chores.

If your garden is well-established you might now look to details of the layout that were not successful during seasons past. Introducing two or three steps into a gentle slope, for example, to change the emphasis of the layout, or replacing a small area of lawn near the house with consolidated gravel for a more relaxed look.

But if your garden requires a complete rethink now is the time for taking tape, pencil and rule, measuring your plot to scale and then drawing a simple plan. Start by plotting the walls, doors and windows of the house, then measure away from it at right-angles to include out-buildings, edges of paving, existing trees and shrubs and planting areas, and finally the boundaries and gateways. Work on tracing paper so that you can overlay one version of your plan and simply draw in your new intensions. Mark the directions of views you have or would like, prevailing wind and any other problems.

The two gardens below required new layouts that solved a number of problems that are typical of the country plot. In both cases you can see the original survey side-by-side the replanned layout.

CASE ONE—THE SURVEY
The garden below had been developed strongly at its edges and centered on nothing. New building to the left of the site as we look at it required screening, and a vegetable plot had become too large to manage. An area of grass close to the house presented mowing problems.

THE REVISED PLAN
The new plan includes new thick screen planting to hide the new building, and re-directs the garden towards a view. The patch of grass close to the house is now consolidated gravel with random planting, and the vegetable patch reduced to a more manageable size.

Beeches
Pine
Cherry
New building here
Grass difficult to cut here
Unused shed
Vegetables
Beech hedge
Garage
Border too thin
Too small an area of grass within structures

Loose screen planting
Rough grass with bulbs
Mown lawn
3 Fastigiate hornbeams
Vegetables
Flower border with hedge backing
Consolidated gravel with random planting
Sitting area
Thick screen planting
Steps up
Paving

CASE TWO—THE SURVEY

The large garden, right, had its prime views blocked by hedging, a mixed border, and an unnatural mound made from the spoil from a pond excavation. The pond was separated from the main bulk of the garden and the house surrounds needed rationalizing.

THE REVISED PLAN

In the proposed new garden the spoil from the pond excavations is contoured into more naturalistic shapes, and added to by the spoil from a certain amount of re-shaping of the pool. The central hedge and mixed border have been removed to open up the required views.

Mound of spoil from pond blocking view to hills beyond

Paddock

Pond

Line of view blocked

Mixed border

Hedging

Outbuilding

House

Re-shaped pond

Screen planting

Bridge

Grade out mounds

Rough grass

Fence re-aligned

Gentle mounds with planting

Flowering trees

Cherry surround by bulbs in rough grass

Terrace adjusted

Outbuilding

New border

House

STEMS IN WINTER

One of the most subtle, but nevertheless pleasurable joys of the country garden in winter, is the abundance of colours and textures displayed by branches and stems denuded of their foliage. This selection was taken from my own garden during a stroll in winter sunshine, when the angle of sunlight was low enough to highlight bark patterns, luminous stems, graphic spikes and downy twigs.

Bamboo (Arundinaria viridistriata)
Remarkably delicate canes with
buff stem-sheaths

Spindle tree (Euonymus alatus)
Partially ribbed stems are a bonus after
brilliant autumnal leaf colour

Salix fargesii *A stout, densely-green stem*
that will turn to a deep, shining brown

Violet willow (Salix daphnoides)
A young shoot still covered in its downy bloom

Dogwood (Cornus alba *'Sibirica'*) *Fresh,*
vigorous growth has the brightest red colour

Snow gum (Eucalyptus niphophila)
''Bleached'' bark flake from one of the most beautiful of gums

Stag's horn
sumach (Rhus
typhina) *Has a*
texture reminiscent
of the velvet covering
a stag's antlers

Cider gum (Eucalyptus gunnii) *Bark*
flake naturally curled to reveal deep orange

Stephanandra tanakae *The sepia tint*
of stephanandra's stems is a winter bonus

Contorted hazel (Corylus avellana contorta) *Fascinating twisted stems*

Rubus cockburnianus *The new stems of this shrub have a white, waxy covering*

Coral-bark maple (Acer palmatum senkaki) *New growth is coral red*

Moosewood (Acer pensylvanicum) *Young stems are green before turning deep brown, traced with white*

Rubus tricolor *A young stem covered in chestnut-brown bristles*

Cider gum (Eucalyptus gunnii) *Young stems have an attractive greyish bloom*

Golden willow (Salix alba vitellina) *Fresh growth is a glowing yellow amber*

Bamboo (Arundinaria murielae) *Canes develop from bright green (top) to strong yellow (bottom)*

HOPEFUL SIGNS

Shelley's line, "If Winter comes, can Spring be far behind?", has a particular significance in the country garden. Depending on the severity of the season and the aspect of your site, there will be signs of new growth long before the official end of winter. As soon as sunshine brings the most fragile warmth to sheltered spots, the first shoots start to appear, followed by the earliest flowers of the year. Few leaves are brave enough to show, since sharp frosts are still about, but aconites and snowdrops are made of sterner stuff and show their cheering, defiant blooms even as the last snows are melting. They are followed by the first *Iris stylosa*, by species crocus and that annual wonder, the early-flowering *Narcissus* 'February Gold'. In wild boggy areas there are banks of butterbur (*Petasites hybridus*), with its felty leaves, and in woodland the first shoots of dog's mercury (*Mercurialis perennis*), with hazel (*Corylus* sp.) catkins and pussy willow (*Salix* sp.) Like the first stirrings of a hibernating mammal, the annual natural cycle is bringing the garden slowly back to life.

Naturalized snowdrops (right) *A bank of both single and double forms of snowdrop (*Galanthus nivalis*) is one of the most cheering sights of late winter, here shown with narcissus pushing through.*

Winter aconites (below) *Another winter beauty, the winter aconite (*Eranthis hyemalis*), naturalizes itself in bold drifts. The flowers open in sunshine to produce sheets of deep buttercup-yellow flowers.*

WINTER VEGETABLES

There is nothing like fresh vegetables to preserve the spirits through winter. Leeks, the *Brassica* crops and Swiss chard are plants of architectural beauty while growing, as well as providing ingredients for warming dishes. Roots and tubers are worthwhile if you have the time and space.

Spinach (Spinacia oleracea) *Sow smooth-seeded varieties throughout winter in mild climates*

Brussels sprout (Brassica oleracea gemnifera) *After frost, sprouts are the tastiest of brassicas*

Parsnip (Pastinaca sativa) *A delicious root that is completely frost hardy*

Leek (Allium ampeloprasum) *A stalwart stem for fresh flavor when all else fails*

Turnip (Brassica rapa) *Less hardy than swede but some varieties have edible foliage*

Swede (Brassica napus) *A versatile root that can be left growing until required*

Red Cabbage (Brassica oleracea) *A colorful addition to stews and winter salads*

Perpetual spinach *Mid-summer sowing will provide a succulent winter crop*

Celery (Apium graveolens) *For soups and braising as well as winter salads*

Main-crop Potato (Solanum tuberosum)

Swiss chard (Beta vulgaris) *Use the stems like celery and the leaves like spinach*

Savoy cabbage (Brassica oleracea bullata) *A heart warming, old friend of a vegetable that looks so well growing*

Cauliflower (Brassica oleracea) *Slower-maturing main crop varieties will last into winter in mild climates*

THE NATURAL GARDEN

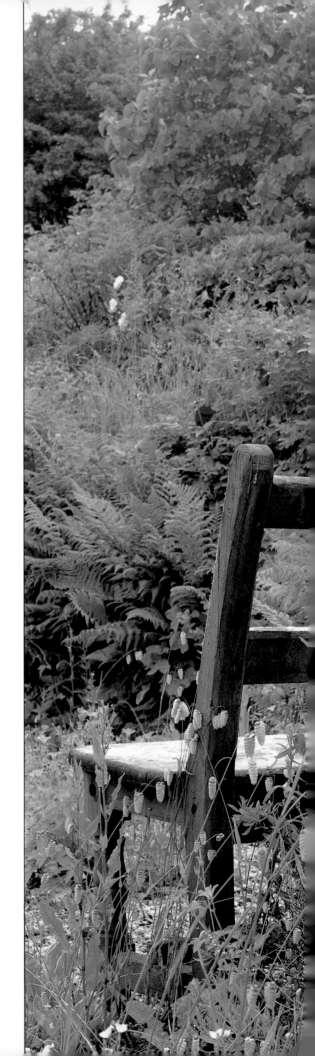

It can be said that all gardens are natural to an extent. But we saw earlier (on pages 14 and 15) how, through different periods of history, styling and layout were decidedly unnatural, in that the plants they contained were restricted and clipped to fit into a classical, formalized ground pattern. Even in the eighteenth century, when styling was much softer, the "landscaped" look was supposed to create an idealized version of nature on a scale where the horticultural element was no smaller than the tree—again hardly natural.

Only in the latter half of the twentieth century, with all the horticultural input of the nineteenth and early twentieth centuries behind us, do we find ourselves re-assessing our situation more practically and considering a new form of garden style, which I shall call the natural garden. Such a style is essentially rural, although elements of it can of course be re-interpreted in an urban location. It is carefully designed to serve the family that uses it, having significant portions in which costly maintenance is minimal. The planting style is relaxed in appearance and, being partly derived from indigenous vegetation, is attractive to native fauna. It is constructed (as far as possible) in the idiom of the structure it surrounds and mindful of styles beyond its boundaries, so that, as a whole, the garden is a welcome addition to its locality rather than a horticulturalized embarrassment. Some tradition-alists might be shocked at the absence of weed-free earth, edged and stripped lawns, manicured, mop-headed trees, and blasts of annual color in the natural garden. If they look a second time, however, they will find a garden at peace with its landscape, alive with softer pleasures and, in its midst, a relaxed and happy gardener.

Careful detailing
Natural garden style calls for relaxed, almost haphazard-looking detailing that is in fact carefully planned. The two voluptuous examples shown here include: a simple, unpainted garden bench (right), couched amongst the delicate, nodding heads of quaking-grass, species gladioli and a grouping of ferns; and foreground anaphalis (left) with pink towering spikes of digitalis.

NATURAL PLANTING

The natural garden look depends greatly on its planting style. It should broadly follow the zone system discussed on page 28, with the more alien species planted in the shelter of the house and/or outbuildings, then a central transitional zone, before there is a blending of plants with native species beyond the boundary.

PLANTING SCALE
The scale of the plants you use should also alter with zone. When adjacent to any structure, plant scale should relate to it, but be generally small including specimens with some architectural form to tie in with the form of the building. Most, however, should provide a considered profusion that softens the look of the structure.

In the boundary zone, on the other hand, masses of the more native species should be in scale with their backdrop, bold swathes in sympathy with distant woods, a hillside or a checkered field pattern. And in between these, in the intermediate zone, a subtle transition.

Looking at the examples of natural garden planting on these pages, it may be difficult to imagine the jump from theory to practice when it comes to achieving that rampant look. The answer is to develop the planting technique that I call "drift and flow" (see p.68). It approximates the naturally-occurring effect of plant drifts and will create the relaxed, (some call it "weedy") look, ideal for the natural garden.

The successful natural-style country gardener comes to understand the plants he or she uses, noting their rates of growth, how they reproduce and how successful they are at it. It then becomes clear that some plants can be left to grow and multiply willy-nilly without the fear of total invasion, while others, those with vigorous root systems, need equally vigorous cutting back and root restriction.

Soft jungle of forms (right) *Verbascum, fennel and digitalis, in the foreground, mixed casually with alchemilla, lavender and evening primrose beyond, are here established in gravel.*

Garden incorporated with the countryside *The harmony between decorative planting and transitional planting between the garden building, the duck pond and the field beyond, epitomizes natural style in this garden.*

DRIFT AND FLOW EFFECT

The drift and flow effect of planted masses starts out in a far from casual way. Once established it will of course fill out, and to a degree alter, since the perennial groups get broader and the bienniels self-seed and come up unexpectedly. But the range of plants that you wish to grow has to be planted out and established, including a skeleton framework of shrubby material. It is this skeleton grouping that prevents the effect from becoming a mess and continues to provide form and interest through the winter when much perennial material will have died down.

You now work down in scale, choosing perennials, biennials and finally annuals, starting with those plants that have the strongest forms. For a plant's form (its overall growth, shape, and the texture of its leaves) is with you far

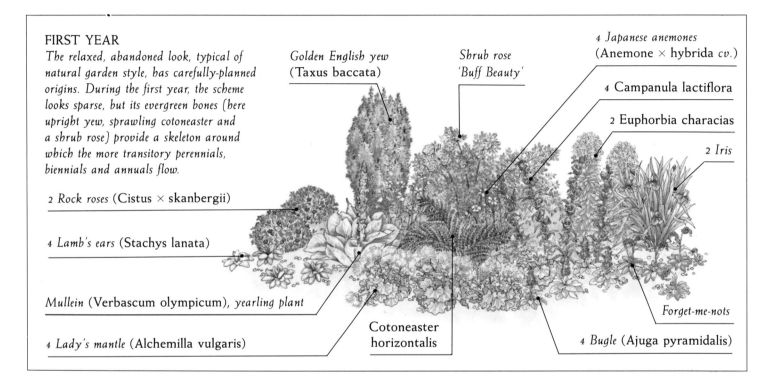

FIRST YEAR
The relaxed, abandoned look, typical of natural garden style, has carefully-planned origins. During the first year, the scheme looks sparse, but its evergreen bones (here upright yew, sprawling cotoneaster and a shrub rose) provide a skeleton around which the more transitory perennials, biennials and annuals flow.

2 Rock roses (Cistus × skanbergii)

4 Lamb's ears (Stachys lanata)

Mullein (Verbascum olympicum), *yearling plant*

4 Lady's mantle (Alchemilla vulgaris)

Golden English yew
(Taxus baccata)

Shrub rose
'Buff Beauty'

4 Japanese anemones
(Anemone × hybrida *cv.*)

4 Campanula lactiflora

2 Euphorbia characias

2 Iris

Forget-me-nots

4 Bugle (Ajuga pyramidalis)

Cotoneaster
horizontalis

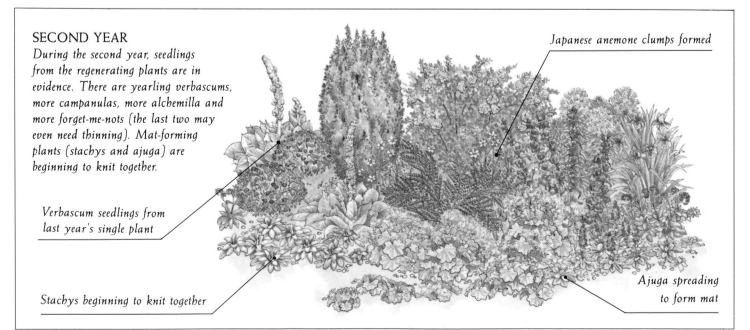

SECOND YEAR
During the second year, seedlings from the regenerating plants are in evidence. There are yearling verbascums, more campanulas, more alchemilla and more forget-me-nots (the last two may even need thinning). Mat-forming plants (stachys and ajuga) are beginning to knit together.

Verbascum seedlings from last year's single plant

Stachys beginning to knit together

Japanese anemone clumps formed

Ajuga spreading to form mat

longer than its flower color. This is not to say that at the back of your mind you are not thinking about an eventual color range *as well*.

Plot your selected plants on paper, envisioning in your mind's eye the finished effect in elevation while drawing it in plan. Use groups of plants (some people only work with odd numbers, but I don't think it matters), drifting a group of six or seven of this with three or five of that. Allow each plant enough space to grow to its preferred size, starting with the large things and working down to the small.

There are two further rules: firstly, select plants from commercial catalogues only (the plant dictionaries are excellent too, but to be practical they must be used in conjunction with listings that represent a real source); and secondly, when you think you have finished your plan, take out half the types of plant you had first considered and double up on the number of the remaining types. We all use too much variety, weakening the visual impact of each plant type by planting too few specimens and providing them with too much competition.

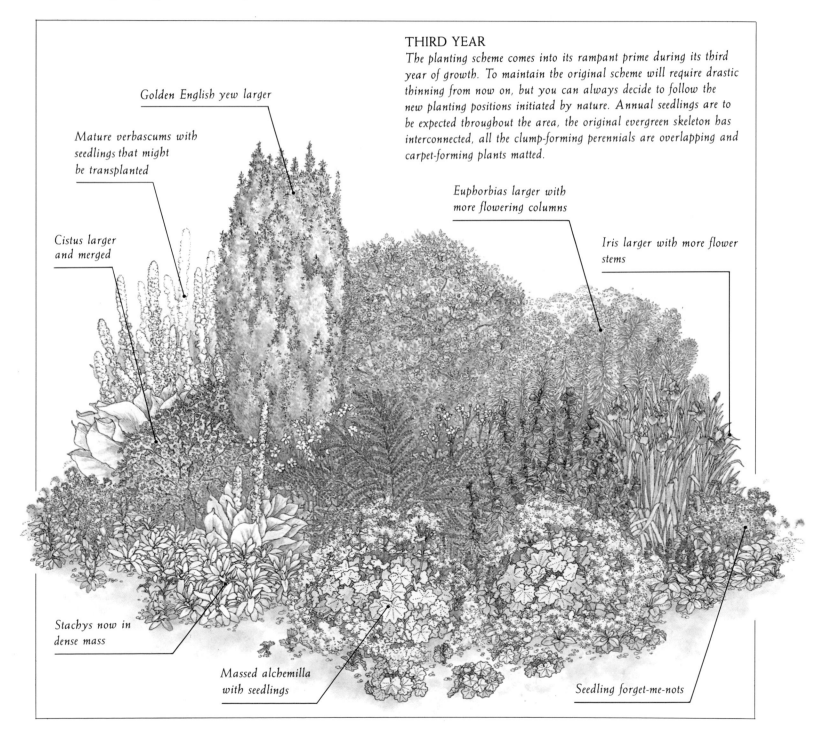

THIRD YEAR

The planting scheme comes into its rampant prime during its third year of growth. To maintain the original scheme will require drastic thinning from now on, but you can always decide to follow the new planting positions initiated by nature. Annual seedlings are to be expected throughout the area, the original evergreen skeleton has interconnected, all the clump-forming perennials are overlapping and carpet-forming plants matted.

Golden English yew larger

Mature verbascums with seedlings that might be transplanted

Euphorbias larger with more flowering columns

Cistus larger and merged

Iris larger with more flower stems

Stachys now in dense mass

Massed alchemilla with seedlings

Seedling forget-me-nots

NEGLECTED CORNERS

We all tend to be too sophisticated in our plant selections. A good source of ideas for more natural plant groups, if not nature herself, is a good and preferably neglected rubbish dump. One longs to see behind the garden door of a manicured period garden to those areas left for compost, sweepings and prunings, to see what has grown of its own accord and what its neighbor might be. The neglected corners of an old garden are often full of incidental plant associations. Sometimes they overlay a previous conscious planting design. To a degree, such natural accidents are the charm of the "olde worlde" garden, but conscious efforts to achieve the same look can be too clever by half. The accidents are an inevitable feature of the natural country garden and can be regarded as a delightful visual bonus. But if you wish to recreate such accidental plant groupings, look at the examples below for ideas.

Natural-looking association *A purple-leaved grape (*Vitis vinifera purpurea*) creeps up a dead tree trunk, and through it a clematis has established itself to make a wonderfully decorative association.*

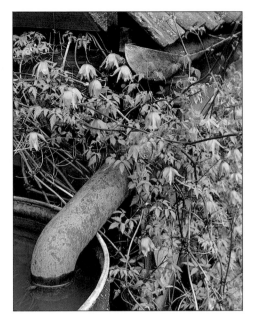

Forgotten niche *The perennial sweet pea (Lathyrus latifolius) frames a casual grouping of potted house-leeks (Sempervivum sp) with a climbing rose and clematis foliage.*

Neglected outhouse *A pink clematis has associated itself with variegated ivy and a sheet of blue campanula, heuchera leaves and a fern, all against a sandstone wall.*

Around a water butt *An old, brimming water butt and down spout forms a dilapidated, but charming, support for a rambling, pink-flowering clematis.*

Defunct workings *Racemes of purple wisteria frame the stone sluice support above an old, and now defunct, weir stop-cock. If you are lucky enough to have such an incidental feature in your garden, its visual attributes will only increase as plants grow around it.*

DISTRESSING TECHNIQUES

The techniques for creating the soft, old-established look that epitomizes the natural garden might be termed distressing, in the same way that there are decorating techniques, using paint for example, to distress walls or woodwork. In the garden, the aim is to soften newly-built or hard-looking surfaces and structures using plant material.

The natural garden design should allow for full and luxuriant planting in association with buildings and paving. It is a good idea to establish an architecturally striking plant as a feature of this planting. Acanthus and euphorbias are particular favorites of mine for this role.

TECHNIQUES FOR PAVING

There are various sources of inspiration for the distressed look as far as paving is concerned. The effect of moss on stone in permanently damp areas is wonderful, but potentially lethal if allowed to develop across paving used as a thoroughfare. Neglected paved yards become overrun in a multitude of attractive ways. Aspects of these looks can be achieved in a designed ground plan that allows for grass growing between slabs or stones; you can use a power mower to occasionally trim the grass and so control the look (see p.41).

Many gardeners try to achieve the look by planting alpines among paving, but if the mass of plants is too varied and unnatural in its placement, it creates an

Using plant associations *You can achieve a distressed look by introducing unexpected combinations. Here annual cosmos is seen with the huge glaucous leaves of one of the kale family between a shrub rose and a conifer.*

SHORT CUTS TO RUIN

Plants in unusual places *The distressed look is based on the softening visual effect that plants have on buildings and paving. Look around you and you will see all kinds of examples of plants colonizing man-made structures. House-leeks (Sempervivum Sp.) establish themselves in the most unlikely of places. Where stone is used as a roofing material, for example, they will make attractive outcrops across a shaded roof. You can simulate this natural effect by establishing house-leeks in a simple wire-netting basket, lined with sphagnum moss and filled with a half-and-half mix of soil-based compost and grit. Attach wires and secure the basket by hooking them under convenient tiles.*

Wall folly *You can even build your own ruined pile if you are committed to the distressed look! Use a few second-hand, local bricks to build a section of walling, saving broken ones to make a crumbling edge. Render the lower courses, leaving a jagged upper edge (you can always hack this away if you are not satisfied with the degree of ruin). Leave for a week, then paint all the surfaces with well-rotted manure solution. Fill any crevice or revealed frog (the hollow of a brick, not the croaking sort) with a little soil-based compost, and then plant with stonecrops.*

unsettling and spotty effect. A visually stronger effect can be achieved by sticking entirely to aubrieta or *Polygonum vaccinifolium* or *Sedum acre* or creeping thyme.

TECHNIQUES FOR WALLS AND ROOFS

Vertical surfaces can be distressed as well, most simply by choosing the right climbing plants—ivy, certain honeysuckles, Boston-ivy, or the beautiful climbing *Hydrangea petiolaris* (for a shady location)—and providing complementary supports.

On a smaller scale, however, plants can be introduced between the stones or bricks of a wall. Wallflowers prefer such a location, while forms of campanula and the little pink perennial erigeron can be grown in this way.

The secret of success is to be able to sustain the correct amount of moisture in the wall. Many old walls were built without a dampproof course and, depending on the porosity of their brick or stone, took up water from the earth like blotting paper; they will sustain plant material. Old brick walls will probably have been built using lime mortar which, being softer than modern cement mortar, is a medium in which seedlings will establish themselves—albeit to the ultimate detriment of the wall.

With new walls, you must either choose a method of construction that allows moisture into the structure, such as dry-stone walling, or build-in planting pockets where a little peat will retain moisture. Double-thickness brick wall construction lends itself to having the gap between the two thicknesses of bricks filled with a peat-based mixture.

Where damp walls are undesirable you can resort to attaching containers to the surface of the wall. In areas where stone is used for roofing, house-leeks (*Sempervivum* sp.) are a natural feature, clinging precariously to crevices. To establish such a group artificially, wire a small netting planter (as shown on page 72) to a shady part of the roof, plant small house-leeks in it, and keep it moist.

Much of the charm of old-established country buildings results from lichen and moss growth on walls and roofs. It can be encouraged prematurely by painting new stone, brick or tiles with diluted cow manure or a solution of milk, but you will have to suffer the temporary smell!

A sense of forgotten romance (left) *Natural garden styling can convey a strong sense of lost romance. Here an inviting doorway is flanked by a bank of white honesty and a carpet of perennial geraniums.*

Rambling charm (above right) *Shade-tolerant blue cranesbill (Geranium 'Johnson's Blue') grows in a haphazard way beneath orchard fruit trees in a charming natural garden.*

Incidental feature (below right) *Are the rocks just a visual pleasure or a seat in this Kentish garden? They are both and, couched in a mixed planting, provide a serendipitous sculptural feature.*

THE RUGGED GARDEN

Within the overall concept of the natural country garden look there are subdivisions that are styled by the conditions imposed by specific locations. One of these is the coast, where many country gardeners battle not only with winds, but with salt-laden ones that sculpt every element of their garden and create a rugged beauty. Here you must use plants that will tolerate blown salt and sand, such as euonymus and elaeagnus, with thrift (*Armeria maritima*), or sea buckthorn (*Hippophae rhamnoides*) and others suited to your coastal climate.

GROUND-HUGGING FORMS

On marginal farming land or moorland there is another rugged look that is inspired by natural rock that might occur within gardens. As on the coast, the wind will often have shaped the land forms, giving trees a characteristic look and rounding the masses of heather or gorse until they too look like rocks. Other plant species native to this kind of dramatic location will have developed a ground-hugging form, growing in carpeting clumps, such as blueberry (*Vaccinium* sp.) and junipers.

CLIMATIC EFFECTS

It is not just the wind that molds the rugged garden, for the associated temperature is all-important. Native coniferous vegetation, heathers and gorses (*Ulex* sp.) have adapted to rugged garden locations where the cold can be intense. Warmer wind-blown areas support other plants with leaf adaptations, such as broom (*Cytisus* sp.), while the oil content of many herbs is an adaptation originally developed as a protection against the doubly drying combination of sun and wind.

Rounded forms (right)
*Wind has rounded the rocks, a sycamore-maple (*Acer pseudoplatanus*), and a fleshy-leaved Griselinia littoralis in a rugged coastal garden.*

Craggy pines (left) *Pine trees make excellent wind breaks, becoming craggy and rugged with age. These sculptural tree trunks are of the Monterey pine (*Pinus radiata*).*

There are many subtleties to the rugged garden by the sea. Within sheltered valleys running down to the sea, the wind-rounded forms that are such a striking feature of exposed coastal gardens give way to an exciting range of plants, including daisy bush (*Olearia* sp.) and the many forms of pittosporum and even fuchsias. These more decorative plants will thrive in the intensity of light reflected from the sea and benefit from the frost-free pocket that will probably exist there.

Other coastal locations, often a little further inland, or on an estuary, are part of a plain that stretches flat to the sea. They suffer the buffeting of salt-laden winds and give the impression of being *on* their landscape, rather than *in* it. The scale of sky and sea demand a tough garden style.

CREATING SHELTER

In any rugged location where salt wind is a problem that reduces your enjoyment of the garden and young plant growth, the most practical and the best visual solution is to plant a belt of native trees and/or shrubs for shelter.

Look to those plants that thrive nearby and would provide a wind break, including tall grasses. Conifers that thrive in maritime and moorland conditions, including Corsican pine, are particularly useful, as are the tough, beautiful thorns (*Crataegus* sp.) and evergreen holm oak (*Quercus ilex*). (For suitable winter-hardy plants for your wind-swept property, consult county extension specialists and of course local nurserymen.)

You could also consider moving a certain amount of earth to build contoured berms to create sheltered pockets within your site. As with all planning for shelter, the art is to balance the need for shelter against the desirability of a view out. An example is shown in the plan, below, of a house with a magnificent view down an estuary, up which comes the prevailing wind. The solution lay in a combination of planting and contouring.

Softer face of the coastal garden (right) *A glorious view of sheltered cottages and gardens across the inlet is afforded from a seaside garden where increased reflected light and shelter from frost allow a luxuriant display of "wild" planting.*

Cliff-top ruggedness (below left) *The beauty of this wind-shaped garden scene would be destroyed by any attempt at decorative gardening.*

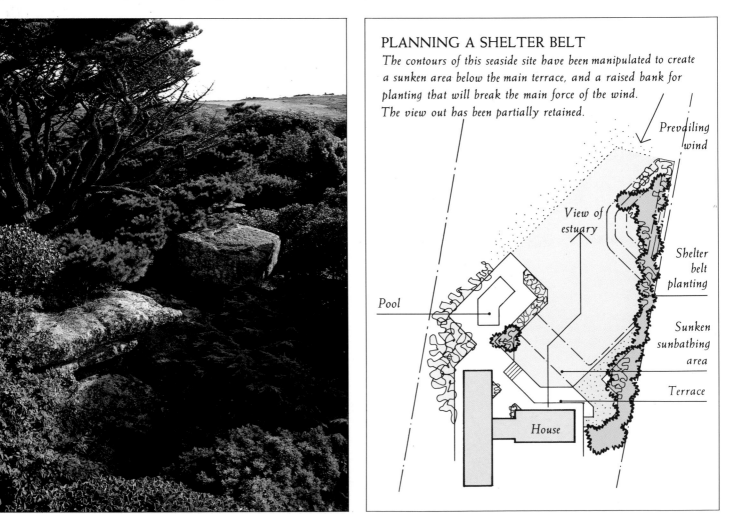

PLANNING A SHELTER BELT

The contours of this seaside site have been manipulated to create a sunken area below the main terrace, and a raised bank for planting that will break the main force of the wind. The view out has been partially retained.

Prevailing wind

View of estuary

Shelter belt planting

Pool

Sunken sunbathing area

Terrace

House

THE QUARRY GARDEN

Another form of rugged garden is inspired by the natural planting that establishes itself among the scree and larger rocks associated with old quarries or rocky upland areas. If your garden is rocky, you should regard the look as a visual bonus and adapt your gardening to suit, rather than attempting a lifetime of clearance.

There is a difference between a rocky look and a garden rockery. The rocky look is essentially a matter of ground shaping with outcrops, while the rockery should appear as solid rock with pockets of earth and general planting associated with it. Garden rockeries are expensive to make, difficult to maintain and have a limited seasonal appeal. For anyone contemplating building one, consider the idea carefully first.

The consideration of outcrops of rock as a sculptural element within the landscape is, however, intriguing, particularly when combined with plants strong enough in their own sculptural form to harmonize.

Rocky look in a valley *The rugged effect of rocks and gravel in this valley garden is enhanced by the bole of a dead tree. Ferns blend with mosses to create a slightly sinister, yet luxuriant, feel.*

The true rockery *A carpet of wild thyme (Thymus serpyllum) growing across huge lichen-covered granite rocks — mineral and vegetable forms blending miraculously together — constitutes a real rockery.*

Coarse granite scree *Forms of potentilla appreciate the hard, though well-drained, medium of coarse granite scree in a Welsh garden. Coarse scree beds are almost maintenance free.*

ROCK FORMATIONS AND PLANTS

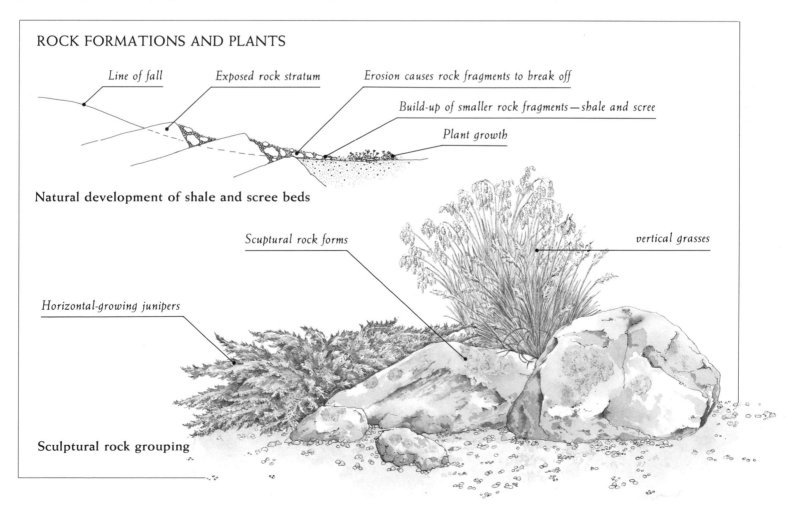

Line of fall

Exposed rock stratum

Erosion causes rock fragments to break off

Build-up of smaller rock fragments — shale and scree

Plant growth

Natural development of shale and scree beds

Scuptural rock forms

vertical grasses

Horizontal-growing junipers

Sculptural rock grouping

WOODLAND GARDEN

One of the most natural forms of garden must be that created within woodland or with a strong woodland feel. Sadly, there is very little native woodland left in Northern Europe that has not been tampered with by man. In North America there is still much native woodland although it is under threat where the land can be exploited commercially. So the study of native woodland has increased, and any remaining pockets of it should be protected at all costs. The country gardener is in the enviable position of being able to add to the woodland total, albeit in a small way, while the town gardener with a country heart will have to rely on planting lower-growing forms of tree and associated plants to create a woodland effect.

TYPES OF WOODLAND GARDEN
Your garden might be inspired by surrounding woodland, or might include within its boundaries some trees and their associated planting. It might be large enough to encompass significant groups of trees, from the smallest grove to woodland big enough for a game covert. It may simply be dominated by one or two standard trees—the sole survivors of an ancient forest.

Whatever your garden's woodland link, you have to be clear about the type of native woodland you are living with and contemplating. Each type will have its predominant type of tree, and then successive natural growth layers beneath. For the gardening element to work visually as well as practically, the plants should be selected to complement these natural layers of vegetation, for example by planting bluebells among hazel trees.

Changing fortunes
(right) *A mixed grouping of mature silver birch, beech and Scots pine, which at one time was part of a northern shelter belt plantation, is now part of an admired garden.*

Small-scale gems (left)
Late autumn cyclamen and early snowdrops make excellent winter ground-cover beneath an oakwood canopy.

What we perceive when looking at native woodland is the climax growth of a whole profile of plants that has taken generations to develop. Just as the natural range of structural materials available for the garden varies according to the local geology, so do plant communities of which trees are the ultimate key members. Native woodland communities can be summarized as follows:

Damp oakwoods grow on deep soils, having a thickish shrub sub-layer often dominated by hazel. In open glades, ash, beech, birch, cherry and hornbeam may grow.

Dry oakwoods grow on coarse sand over sandstone. They include birch and mountain ash, which, together with the dominant oaks, create a close canopy allowing a reduced shrub layer beneath.

Beechwoods grow in chalky (limestone) soils or in loam over chalk and even in acid soils, as long as they are well-drained. Little grows beneath beech, although, if sparsely enough planted, whitebeam and ash may.

Ashwoods may establish themselves in damp chalky soils, often in association with hawthorn.

Pinewoods (natural as opposed to man-made forests) prefer sandy soil. Few plants will grow beneath pines, unless their lower branches have died or been removed.

But how does this knowledge of natural vegetation help the gardener to create a wooded country look on a small scale? It is a salutary thought that most lowland garden locations would have been forest at one time. Before the first city, town, village, hamlet, house, even the first brick, the soil was at one with its trees and their associated plants. You can introduce the spirit of woodland by planting just one or two appropriate trees and associating them with complementary lower planting.

Beech tree trunks (right) *Beech tree trunks have a monumental quality somehow emphasized by a mossy ground cover.*

Spirit of woodland (below) *One or two tree trunks in your garden will evoke the spirit of woodland, especially if you have inherited mature specimens. The two plane trees (Platanus acerifolia), left, are covered in lichen due to the dampness of a seaboard location, while the ancient, braced mulberry (Morus nigra), right—a legacy of the silk trade in England—casts its gnarled charm over a country garden in town.*

FOLIAGE

Two of the many attractive facets of the woodland garden are foliage shape and foliage color. Foliage shape tempers the way light filters through differing densities of leaves; foliage color comes into its own in autumn. With many trees, the intensity of leaf color in autumn varies according to the amounts of sunlight and rainfall they receive through the preceding summer, but certain trees never fail to display. Among "wilder" species, silver birch (*Betulus* spp.), field maple (*Acer campestre*), beech (*Fagus* spp.), hornbeam (*Carpinus* spp.) and wild cherry (*Prunus avium*) color best, with various forms of viburnum in the shrub layer beneath their canopy. But many exotic species can be associated with them, with discretion, to give a range of color from lemon yellow through chrome, to gold, russet and deepest purple.

Two woodland walks (right and below) *Autumn in a garden full of deciduous trees is a visual delight of changing leaf color. The bulk of mature trees, and the way their shapes interlock, creates seclusion and a sense of calm in a relatively small space.*

SPINNEYS AND COPSES

The dictionary description of a spinney is a small grove of trees, while a copse (or coppice) is a wood of small growth for periodical cutting or "coppicing". The term spinney does not evoke dense growth, but rather a sparse planting of standard trees, with open glades of younger shrubby plants beneath. New spinneys may be planted with any number of trees, although for relatively quick decorative effect, stick to forest-scale trees, and do not mix the species too heavily. Traditionally, flowering trees occurred at the edge of the mix, and those with autumn color and/or fruit extend the spinney's interest. Species of *Malus* (the crab apples) are excellent.

The copse is a traditional form of land management in damp oakwood areas (see p. 84) where hazel (*Corylus* sp.) is planted at close intervals and periodically cut back to ground level to form a "stool". The growth removed includes many stems as thick as a broomhandle that are used to weave into hurdles. These were once used to temporarily enclose grazing sheep but now make excellent fencing material for the country garden. From a gardening point of view, developing a few hazel, dogwood or willow stools will ensure fresh, vigorous growth and strong autumn leaf color and will create a woodland feeling even in a very small area.

PLANTING A COPSE

Where a wooded boundary is becoming too tall — with an undesirable view beneath the tree foliage canopy developing — you might consider planting a younger spinney, both as a foreground feature and as a way of increasing the effectiveness of the boundary screen.

In this case the existing planting was of birch with pine and, on the perimeter, the white-flowering Amelanchier lamarckii. *All these are re-used in a circle in front of the originals, the plan allowing for easy fencing while the trees are saplings.*

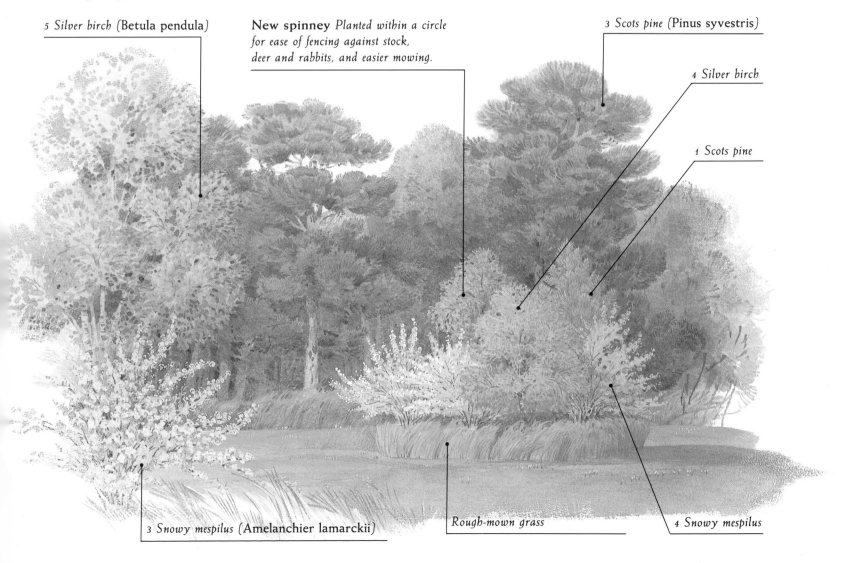

5 *Silver birch* (Betula pendula)

New spinney *Planted within a circle for ease of fencing against stock, deer and rabbits, and easier mowing.*

3 *Scots pine* (Pinus syvestris)

4 *Silver birch*

1 *Scots pine*

3 *Snowy mespilus* (Amelanchier lamarckii)

Rough-mown grass

4 *Snowy mespilus*

THE COLOR GARDEN

For those of us living in the more northerly climes, the thought of color outside is light at the end of a dark tunnel during the long months of winter. We pore over plant catalogues in anticipation and select a host of ill-assorted shrubs, perennials and annuals to brighten a far off summer scene. The trouble is that, while using color as the chief criterion for the plan of your country garden is a perfectly understandable method, with many models and precedents in the history of gardening, it is a course strewn with pitfalls. The deepest of these is that the hybridization of exotic plant material (anything short of tropical), has given gardeners the possibility of a color palette that would put a fairground in the shade. While it is possible to get away with making a riot of exotic color in a walled town garden—for you have only yourself to blind—in the country it makes more sense to use colors that harmonize with nature's own.

COLOR AND NATURAL GARDENING

Whilst your eye might forgive an exotic plant species in a natural garden, especially if it has a harmonious color as well as form and texture that complement its indigenous backdrop, it is very difficult not to be offended by the violent oranges and purples of many species. Why not include the way you consider color in your new natural country garden perspective, at least towards the boundary of your plot where the color of the plants within your garden should harmonize with the colors outside it?

Do not forget that in many country locations, everything is seen against and within the many shades of green. And early morning,

Gray with silver birch
(right) *This restful, gray foreground of herbs blends very well with silver birch trunks in the middle distance.*

Yellows against a cereal crop (left) *The creams and chrome yellows of foliage variegation and tobacco plant blooms blend perfectly with the harvest gold of a cereal crop in a field beyond the garden.*

sparkling dew-covered green, is quite different from the hazy blue of green in high sunlight, and soft evening light produces yet another tone. So nature's colors themselves are modified by different qualities of light, which should give you a wide tonal range from which to choose the plant material for your country garden.

Whilst the color of the foliage of native trees is broadly green, it too varies in tone from the dark green of some native conifers and yew, which seem almost black on the skyline in winter, to the light gray-green of the whitebeams (*Sorbus* sp). But there is no purple foliage that grows naturally, nor heavily variegated foliage, or that virulent glaucous blue of some introduced conifers.

FLOWER COLOR

The colors of the flowers of the majority of native trees and shrubs are cream, lemon, white or green. Native wild flower color also tends towards these paler colors, moving with the seasons through pinks, pale blues, then yellows and golds. Where nature establishes broad bands of one color (and she does not often mix large masses of color) they tend to be in light shade, such as the bluebell

HEATHER PLANTING SCHEME

The strong purples and mauve/pinks of heather deserve space. This simple scheme brings the colors of a distant moor right into a garden. The shapes of the planting areas within the garden complement nature's "moorland marquetry" (a term coined by the Scottish artist Ian Hamilton Finlay) formed by the combinations of patches of heather contrasted with patches of grassland and woodland.

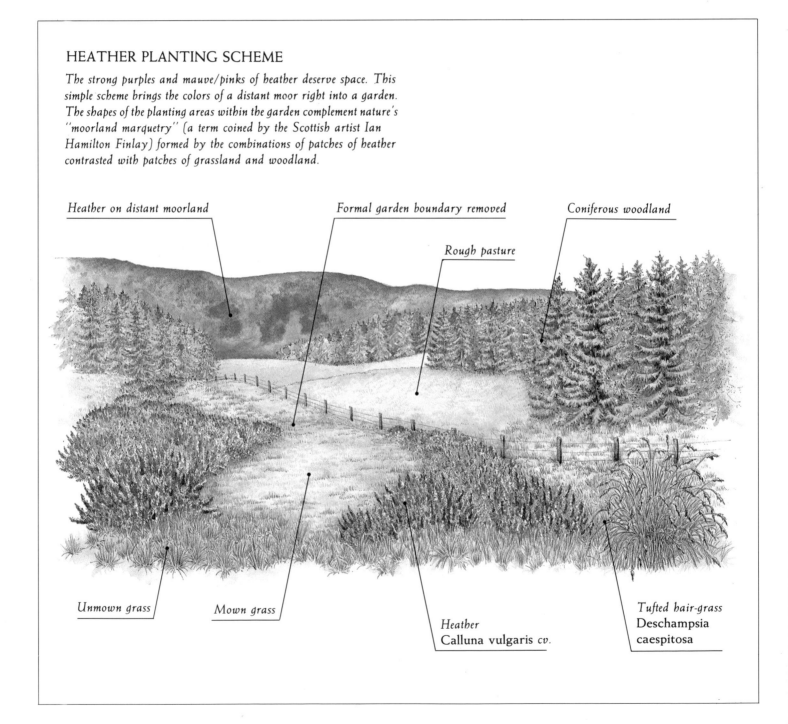

Heather on distant moorland

Formal garden boundary removed

Coniferous woodland

Rough pasture

Unmown grass

Mown grass

Heather
Calluna vulgaris *cv*.

Tufted hair-grass
Deschampsia
caespitosa

mass, or sheets of wild garlic or dog's mercury. Where there is a brilliance of natural color, such as poppies, they usually grow amongst grass or corn, and their amazing color is softened and diluted. It is the diluted color effect—the mosaic of dots of color—that is the essence of cottage garden style (see p.118).

Gertrude Jeckyll, the celebrated early twentieth-century English plantsperson, is often wrongly associated with cottage garden style. For although she admired cottage garden flowers, her use of color was far from diluted, rather she used color and texture as a painter might, in broad swathes. She used hotter colors in the foreground—what I now term the domestic zone A (see p.28)—and linked them to softer blues in the perimeter zone, where they blended into the cool damp light of a typical Edwardian summer's day! The use of color in the garden is very personal, and as different people dress in particular color ranges to suit their personality, their physical characteristics and the fashion of the day, so differing sites and locations, the period of the house, and the activities surrounding it, will dictate suitable color ranges for your plants.

GRASSES PLANTING SCHEME

The scheme below contrasts the horticultural flower color of perennials, planted in a single bold swathe in the foreground, with the subdued color of naturalized grasses. The grasses are planned to complement a back-drop of open countryside, near inland water or perhaps adjacent to a seaside inlet.

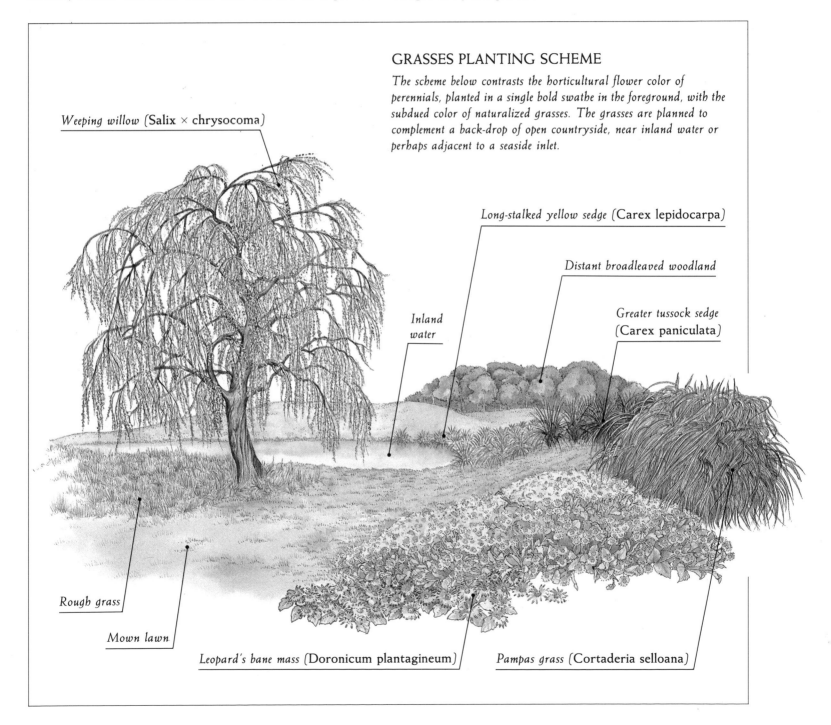

Weeping willow (Salix × chrysocoma)

Long-stalked yellow sedge (Carex lepidocarpa)

Distant broadleaved woodland

Greater tussock sedge (Carex paniculata)

Inland water

Rough grass

Mown lawn

Leopard's bane mass (Doronicum plantagineum)

Pampas grass (Cortaderia selloana)

THE GARDEN IN SPRING

When Browning reminisced, "Oh, to be in England now that April's there", it was not because the weather is particularly good—April can be terrible in Britain—but because there is a delicious expectancy in the air that accompanies the gradual reawakening. After at least two, if not three, months of feeling that winter will never end, the smallest signs of spring relieve the depression and confirm the promise of winter's brave flowers. All at once you notice that the evenings are staying lighter, and daffodils are everywhere. If you keep out of the wind, the sun is actually quite warm again. The lambs are growing fast and the earth is drying out, the birds are making a tumultuous noise in the mornings and suddenly it's fine to cut the grass again!

Another month and most trees are in leaf, even the tulips are here. A haunting cuckoo call carries across the fields and, in the woods, bluebells push through the groundcover of dog's mercury. It's an enchanted time, when you need to be outside. Little wonder that the pagans danced to celebrate the spring equinox, to convey that winter was finally felt to be dead and buried.

NATURE'S PATTERNS
As wild flowers begin to show in spring, take special note of nature's planting patterns before lusher growth makes them more difficult to discern. Observe the random scatter of primroses along a bank, for example, or the drifts of wild bulbs that have spread over many years. These are the patterns you will want to interpret in your garden as you sow and plant for the year ahead, and for next spring: strengthening an effect here, possibly, and removing a mistake there.

The bluebell wood
(right) *An English bluebell (Scilla non-scripta) wood in May is a classic model for the natural gardener. Sheets of blue carpet the ground beneath beech trees (Fagus sylvatica).*

Wild primroses (left)
The wild primrose (Primula vulgaris) appears on damp mossy banks in early spring. Its purity of color is matched only by its sharp, spicy fragrance.

SPRING FLOWER COLOR

Flowers from bulbs provide the predominant colors in the cultivated spring garden, but in the natural country garden they should simply complement native species, just as the daffodils combine with dandelions (*Taraxacum officinale*) and pale blue speedwell (*Veronica officinalis*) in the photograph opposite.

Unfortunately, hybridization has led to the development of showy plant forms that bear little resemblance to their natural parents. The natural colors of the spring garden are quite subtle—the new greens of tree and grass foliage, for example—and it is all too easy to allow strident cultivated colors to ruin them. Strong pink, for instance, is not a spring color in the wild, where lemon and yellow predominate. Strong blues are usually diffused in a mass of greenery. Save strong-colored bulbs for planting in the proximity of the house and terrace.

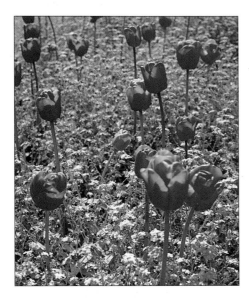

Sugar pink tulips *Such a strong color combination of pink tulips with forget-me-nots is stunning in isolation against a building.*

Narcissus *Choose the smaller kinds for naturalizing. They are more resistant to wind and look perfect in the natual garden.*

Lily-flowered tulips *Lily-flowered tulips are very graceful and provide a delicate compromise between man-made and wild forms.*

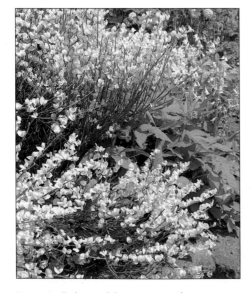

Broom *Cultivated brooms provide a warm splash of delicate spring colour. This is the form Cytisus scoparius 'Sulphureus'.*

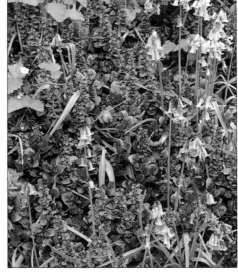

Bugle and bluebells *Bugle with bluebells makes a striking semi-wild spring plant combination for a shaded corner.*

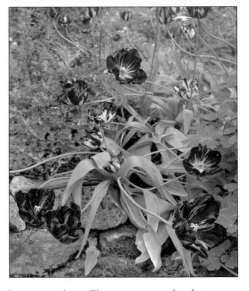

Parrot tulips *Flopping, naturalized parrot tulips with loose petals make a striking feature growing in an old stone wall.*

SPRING BULBS

The earliest spring flowers are those of the bulbs, and
whether they were newly planted last autumn, or are old friends re-appearing
in time-honored fashion, they are equally welcome. This selection of
narcissus, with anemones and some of the blue-flowering bulbs,
has enough natural charm for any country look.

Narcissus 'Golden Ducat' (left)
A mid-season double (in bud)

Narcissus 'Blaris'
A modern daffodil hybrid

Narcissus minor *Perhaps a
form of N.pseudonarcissus,
but to 15 cm (6 in)*

**Narcissus
'Ice Follies'** *Early
spring to mid-spring,
large-cupped narcissus*

**Narcissus 'Telemonius
Plenus'** *A double form
established in Italy
in the 17th century*

**Narcissus
pseudonarcissus**
(above) *This is the
common daffodil
of early spring*

**Narcissus
pseudonarcissus
subsp. moschatus**
*A pale form native
to the Pyrennees*

Narcissus pseudonarciss
(above) *Wild form*

Narcissus 'Hawera'
A delicate hybrid between
N. triandrus *and*
N. jonquilla

Narcissus 'Cragford'
Horticultural form of the
Tazetta narcissus group

Narcissus 'Langwith'
A trumpet narcissus

Narcissus 'Penvose'
Modern daffodil hybrid

Narcissus tazetta *cv.*
Fragrant horticultural form

Grape-hyacinth
(Muscari
armeniacum)
Likes full sun and
well-drained soil

Scilla sibirica
A native of woods,
scrub and screes

Anemone blanda (below)
Best under deciduous
trees in light shade

Anemone blanda
'White splendour'
Flowers as much as
5 cm (2 in) across

Glory-of-the-snow
(Chionodoxa luciliae)
Grows naturally on
stony hillsides

PLANTING FOR SPRING

Most gardeners are conditioned to planting a comparatively limited range of spring bulbs when there is a much wider range available, especially for the country garden. Take the genus *Allium* for instance, species of which start flowering in late spring. They are easy to grow in any light, well-drained soil and prefer a sunny position. Many,

Mixed spring collection (left) *The dappled shade cast by small trees provides ideal conditions for dog's tooth violet amongst* Arum pictum *and a sheet of blue muscari.*

particularly the smaller forms, (*A. moly* and *A. azureum* for example) increase themselves rapidly and are therefore excellent plants to establish in gravel (see p. 104).

Anemones are excellent for the semi-wild look. *Anemone apennina* and *A. blanda* (see p. 97) both do well in sun or light shade, and increase and ramble in light woodland. The true woodland anemone is *A. nemerosa* and it prefers a damp situation.

Chionodoxa or glory-of-the-snow has charming clear blue flowers—so named because they bloom as the snow

PLANTING SCHEME FOR A GRAVEL OASIS WITH SPRING-FLOWERING BULBS

A birch grove can make a wonderful transition from garden to countryside, and is the ideal location for various naturalized, *spring-flowered bulbs. Here is a planting scheme for bulb masses between silver birches on either side of a gravel path.*

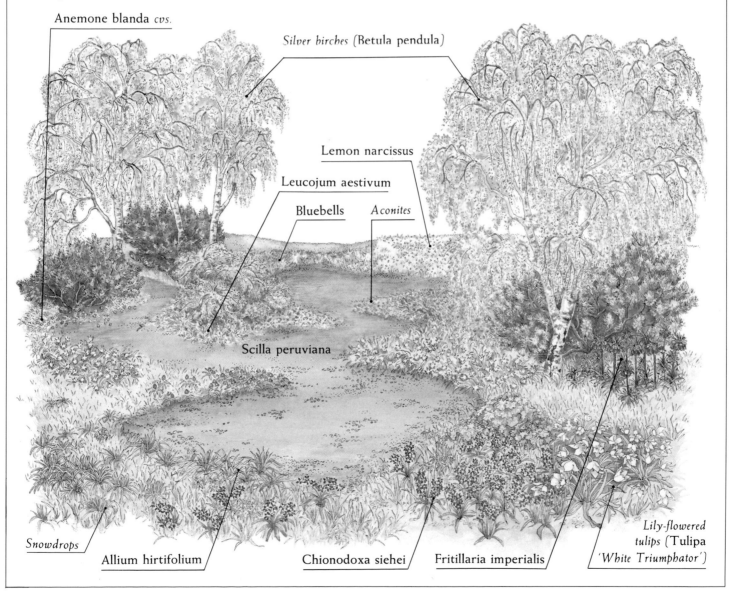

Anemone blanda *cvs.*

Silver birches (Betula pendula)

Lemon narcissus

Leucojum aestivum

Bluebells

Aconites

Scilla peruviana

Snowdrops

Allium hirtifolium

Chionodoxa siehei

Fritillaria imperialis

Lily-flowered tulips (Tulipa 'White Triumphator')

melts in the mountains of Turkey. It likes the sun and good drainage and is therefore an ideal gravel bulb. Plant them in association with the similarly blue-flowered *Scilla spp,* which will spread themselves rapidly.

Flowers of the dog's tooth violet genus, *Erythronium,* are real eye-stoppers in damp semi-shade. Their foliage, as well as their unusual flowers are excellent.

The fritillaries, with their bell-like flowers, are plants around which fairy stories could be written. There are visual goodies and baddies amongst them. The goodies are the delicate little snake's head fritillaries (*Fritillaria meleagris*), which have unparalleled charm when established in grass and do best in semi-shaded conditions. The baddies are the crown imperials, *F. imperialis,* which have great stately heads of hanging flowers (either yellow or orange red) and prefer sun and loam.

TULIPS

Species tulip,of which there are many forms, flower earlier than the ubiquitous forms of bedding tulip in the main and are much smaller. Many (*Tulipa clusiana* and *T. tarda,* for example) have flowers which open fully like lilies in sun. The Greigii hybrids also have beautiful striped foliage. To naturalize tulips, you have to plant bulbs at least 15cm (6 in) deep in a well-drained soil, preferably in sun. Over a period of years, the size of naturalized plants and their flowers decrease, but this process often increases their natural charm.

AFTER THE BULBS

As the bulb flowers begin to die, springtime moves on to scenes of lambs under orchard blossoms—the very soft pink flowers of apple and pear. Natural tree blossoms, including cherry (*Prunus avium*), the bird cherry (*Prunus padus*), wild crab apple (*Malus sylvestris*) and blackthorn (*Prunus spinosa*), are all white sometimes turning to cream. As with bulb flowers, sugar pink and red blossoms have an alien look and have to be used very carefully in the overall scene, especially if backed by landscape. It is best to avoid them or to use them against darker coniferous greens for maximum effect.

Tulips for border planting (right) *Tulips can be a very successful ingredient in a mixed border scheme. This pink and yellow combination is backed by irises, hostas and bergenias.*

Cherry blossoms (below) *The particularly fine cherry,* Prunus 'Ukon', *framing a view across the lawn in my garden, has pale yellow semi-double flowers that blend with the fresh green foliage of spring.*

SPRING BLOSSOMS

The joy of seeing the first blossom unfurling from bursting
buds is undiminished no matter how many times you
have seen it before. It affirms the health of the garden
as it stirs itself from winter's sleep, and its transient
beauty and fragrance is a promise of fruits to come.

Common pear (Pyrus communis)
*Cultivated pears are
indistinguishable from
wild ones*

Lilac (Syringa ×
diversifolia) *A
hybrid whose panicles
of white flowers are
particularly early*

Blackthorn or sloe
(Prunus spinosa) *Small
white flowers usually
precede the leaves*

Siberian crab (Malus
baccata), left.
*The delicate white blossom
of a naturalized species
of crab apple*

Bird cherry
(Prunus padus)
*Fragrant flowers are born
in spreading racemes*

Cherry laurel (Prunus laurocerasus)
*Racemes of tiny, creamy white flowers
seen against shiny green leaves*

Cultivated cherry (Prunus
'Ukon'), right. *Semi-double
flowers tinted yellowish-green*

Cultivated cherry (Prunus
'Shirofugen'), above.
*Double flowers, the
palest of pinks in bud,
white on opening*

Snowdrop tree
(Halesia carolina)
*A beautiful north
American native
with creamy, bell-
shaped flowers*

Plum (Prunus domestica *'Plantierensis'*)
*The creamy white blossom of this double-
flowered form of plum*

Gean cherry (Prunus
avium *'Plena'*) *Profusely
flowering, snowy white form*

THE GRAVEL GARDEN

Gravel is being used increasingly as a ground-covering medium having a number of advantages. Texturally, it is an intermediate between the hard pavings — brick, stone and concrete — and the softness of grass. Design-wise it works as a transition between the two, making both an all-weather, practical surfacing and, with plants, a decorative space as well. An area of gravel can be seen as another element within the collage of your overall garden design too (see p.40), linking visually with, say, the house structure and outbuildings, or perhaps just the garden wall that it adjoins.

The proliferation of sit-on mowers which need wide turning circles and cannot negotiate tight corners, has created many an awkward country garden corner, ideal for gravel surfacing.

CONSOLIDATED CONSTRUCTION TECHNIQUE

The gravel surfacing that I advocate is not the sort of soft and crunchy morass that clings like a bog (although as a burglar deterrent in certain situations this is not a bad idea); it is hard and consolidated, similar to a French market place on which the locals play *boules.* If necessary, the surface should be retained by a curb such as brick-on-edge.

To create such an area, excavate to approximately 75mm (3 in) depending on your soil — more for clay and sand, less for flint or stones. Roll and consolidate into this 60mm (2½ in) of unwashed gravel or ballast. This will have clay amongst it and it will bind together with moisture to become hard. Into this roll and consolidate the top layer of finished, preferably rounded, pea shingle — the type of gravel that has been dug from pits and smoothed by the action of water. This medium

Gravel as a foil (right)
Not only is well-consolidated gravel a first-rate surface to walk on, it also serves as a fine visual foil to plants with strong form.

Self-seeders (left)
Annual orange California poppies (Eschscholzia sp.) self-seed in gravel and combine well with golden feverfew (Chrysanthemum parthenium).

is kinder to small children if they fall over in it. However, in areas where there is a naturally occurring stone, you will find the local gravel is a quarried version of it. Although the medium will be sharper-edged, it will be a perfect visual match to your local materials.

The finished, rolled surface will be semi-porous and over a period, dust will collect in it and weeds will inevitably self-seed. But if these will regenerate and flourish, so will masses of garden plants and it is the random, woolly effect which this surfacing encourages that is so attractive.

Maintenance could not be more simple. When the weedy look gets too much for you, simply hoe through the top surface of gravel on a hot, sunny day so that unwanted growth is cut away or uprooted, then dries and dies. The odd out-of-place seedling can be weeded out by hand. Light raking and the occasional top dressing with fresh gravel will revive "tired" areas.

Gravelled corner *The thistle, Eryngium giganteum 'Miss Wilmott's Ghost', is a great self-seeder. Here it is growing in gravel together with hollyhocks.*

COUNTRY COURTYARD PLANTING SCHEME

Planted gravel areas are particularly successful close to or between buildings. Arranged in a seemingly random way, the planting takes on a cottagey feel, here to be seen against a pink-washed wall.

1 *Loquat* (Eriobotrya japonica)

1 *Smoke bush* (Cotinus coggyria 'Atropurpurea')

6 *White-flowering* Iris unguicularis

1 *White-flowering* Wisteria venusta

1 Acanthus mollis

1 *Rheum palmatum 'Rubrum'*

1 Viburnum plicatum 'Lanarth'

Viola labradorica *mass*

Candytuft mass (Iberis saxatilis)

New Zealand burr mass (Acaena anserinifolia)

3 *Oregon grape* (Mahonia aquifolium 'Atropurpureum')

Lily-of-the-Valley mass (Convallaria majalis)

PLANTING IN GRAVEL

As well as waiting for the natural self-seeding of plants in the dust build-up in gravel surfacing, you can create planting pockets within the medium and so establish the natural look very quickly.

Take a crowbar and pierce the newly-laid gravel and its consolidated base, to make a hole that you can enlarge with a spade. Backfill this hole with fertile soil, planting your subject as you do so. Include the odd woody plant that will enjoy the well-drained conditions, perhaps a rose or a dwarf conifer. Many herbs and gray-foliaged perennials will also thrive happily in gravel.

Where the gravel is prevented from spilling into planting areas by a curb, plants will naturally spread out and disguise the edging. However, the edging can be further blurred by planting at random through the gravel on the "wrong" side of the curb.

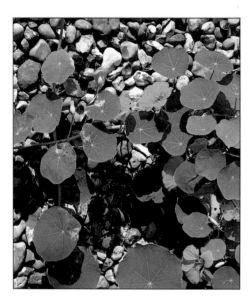

Nasturtiums *The dwarf annual varieties of the genus* Tropaeolum, *will pop up through a dry gravel medium, and continue to self-seed.*

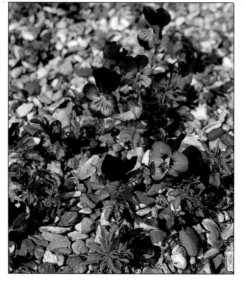

Johnny-jump-up *These tiny pansies* (Viola tricolor), *though short-lived, self-sow freely, especially in gravel.*

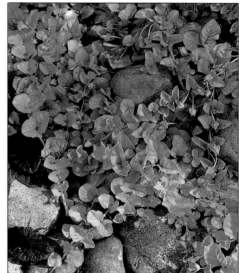

Lysimachia nummularia 'Aurea' *Creeping Jenny is a delightful specimen for gravel. This example has bright gold foliage.*

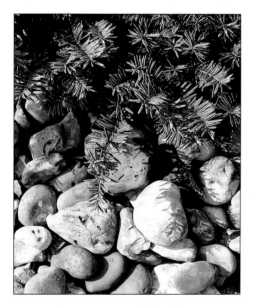

Taxus 'Repens Aurea' *The low-growing, golden variegated yew makes a good evergreen skeleton shrub through gravel.*

Verbascum olympicum *Felty rosettes represent the yearling plants of this biennial, which will develop a yellow flower spike.*

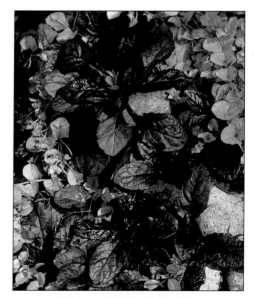

Ajuga reptans 'Atropurpurea' *Makes a good groundcover in partial shade, having blue flower spikes in early summer.*

THE FLOWER GARDEN

Having considered the use of color in the country garden (the rules for which apply just as much to foliage as to flowers), let us look at the various forms of flower-only gardening and see how they fit into the country garden today. For many gardeners the quantity of flowers in any garden is still the criterion by which the excellence of that garden is judged; but they are missing so much else. The numerous horticultural publications, public authorities and plant merchants' catalogues encourage people to regard blast upon blast of randomly mixed, garish flower colors as the gardener's only goal.

Such an attitude belittles the natural beauty of flowers, which, in their native or less hybridized forms have a balance of shape, structure, color and often a fragrance, that combine to provide one of life's great delights. The unthinking use of ever bigger and brighter blooms only detracts from each individual specimen's attributes and overshadows the gentler charms of native flowers.

SYMPATHETIC USE OF FLOWER COLOR

The natural country garden calls for a use of flower color that reserves brighter displays for schemes to be seen in association with buildings. Elsewhere in the garden it must complement local indigenous planting, especially where flowers will be seen against the country backdrop. Using wild flowers exclusively is a form of gardening that is gaining great popularity (see p.116).

Where a bright, mixed flower garden is inappropriate, and you want to grow flowers for cutting, you might consider using them in rows or blocks as in a vegetable garden, where they can look spectacular.

Massed flowers used successfully (right) *Massed flowers can be spectacularly successful when used in a definite color scheme, especially when seen against buildings, such as this French farmhouse.*

Flowers in the kitchen garden (left) *Surely no more pleasant job exists than cutting flowers on a summer morning? Here larkspur and delphiniums are being cut for drying from massed ranks in the kitchen garden.*

ROSES

Few climates allow a longer flowering period for roses than does that of the United Kingdom, where many roses will bloom all summer—and that is unique. Most other places in the world have late spring and early summer roses—but the flowers do not last further into the year. So it is not surprising that the rose is very much part of the English summer flower garden scene.

The rose garden *per se* is now something of a period concept, for it assumes that outside the rose blooming season there are other parts of the garden to which one can go. Nowadays, it is more pertinent to recognize that there are types of *Rosa* that combine excellently with other plants in the mixed border.

OLD-FASHIONED FORMS FOR NEW GARDENS

For myself, the type of rose that best fits into the more natural garden is undoubtedly the shrub rose, a large category that encompasses various types including wild roses, traditional old garden roses and modern shrub roses—a grouping of roses that I collectively term old-fashioned. The newer shrub roses have an extended flowering period, which the older ones did not, though their "improved" flower forms may come at the expense of their fragrance.

Most important, however, is that shrub roses in the main grow into a bush shape that has character, with the added advantage of colored hips in the autumn. Shrub roses can look well simply as specimen shrubs amongst rough grass, or used as part of a hedge, for many have a natural grace, both in and out of flower. The attributes of the plant extend to climbing and rambling forms that will complement old walls or ramble into fruit trees.

Against a shady backdrop (right) *The color of this briar hybrid shrub rose 'Cerise Bouquet' is strengthened when contrasted with a dark, shady backdrop. Its form is open, relaxed and graceful.*

A rose for cutting (below) *This beautiful, pink in bud, white in flower, hybrid tea rose, 'Tamora', has dark glossy foliage and makes an excellent flower for cutting and arranging.*

FLOWERS FOR CUTTING

It is strange that while one's house might be surrounded with flowers in summer, big bunches of flowers, like that opposite (including white shasta daisies, *Echinops ritro* and lavender) are still irresistible for cutting and bringing indoors to put into vases.

Most of us have favorite flowers for cutting. They will have been selected through personal reminiscences, romantic associations, the style of our house interior and,

more practically, what lasts longest in water. It is best to cut flowers in the morning when the dew has gone, but before the sun is hot. This way the stem contains the maximum amount of moisture, and the flowers will be at their best, fully open and not yet drooping. Prior to arranging the flowers in a suitable container, it is a good idea to stand them for a while in deep cool water in the shade, as in the example opposite.

Teasels *One of the loveliest of wild flowers (or fruiting heads) for cutting is Fullers' teasel (Dipsacus fullonum).*

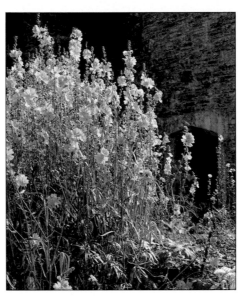

Sidalcea *The tall spires of pink sidalcea, a hardy perennial of the mallow family, make a dramatic contribution to any arrangement.*

Salvia 'Claryssa' *The bright bracts of this annual salvia offer an ever reliable source of cut flowers with country charm.*

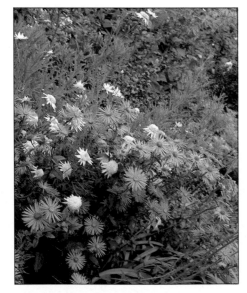

Chrysanthemums and asters *Shasta daisies and various perennial asters are all excellent for cutting.*

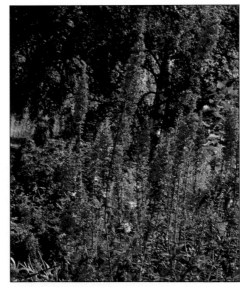

Larkspur cultivars *The huge pink flowerheads of double annual larkspur (Consolida sp.) are excellent cut fresh.*

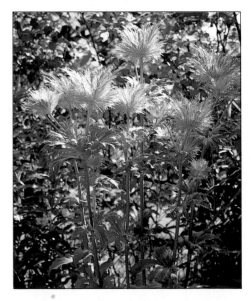

Looking for the unusual *Be on the look out for unlikely flowerheads to spice your displays, such as these heads of echinops.*

WILDFLOWER GARDENING

The romantic associations of wild flowers, their reported demise through the spraying programs demanded by modern forms of agriculture, and the possibility of turning some spare piece of land into something pretty, have combined all of a sudden to popularize the concept of wild-flower gardening. Add to this the ecological favors of protecting the homes of endangered species of bugs, and providing food for your local fauna, and the idea cannot fail to appeal to country gardeners.

However, the reality is something else. If you cultivate a piece of ground and leave it, sooner or later the most invasive of indigenous and nearby naturalized plants will take over. The effect may be decidedly weedy, but in many regions some flowering surprises may appear.

In some rural regions, uncut lawns may become a wildflower meadow, which, with the addition of naturalized spring bulbs, is the most practical sort of wildflower garden for sunny areas. Unfortunately, such casually planned effects may end up a weed patch.

CREATING A WILDFLOWER MEADOW

The wildflower purist who wants a virgin wildflower meadow should consider the work involved. Native grasses in the main grow too vigorously to allow seedling wild flowers to establish themselves, so sprinkling packets of wild flowers in the lawn is not the way. What is required first is the destruction of the existing coarse perennial grasses and any other tenacious plant. It is a paradox that to do this you may have to use the very weedkiller which has destroyed the wild flowers we long to see!

Across this virgin territory you sow a *prepared wildflower and fine grass seed mix*. It is essential that this is suitable for your conditions both for its own well being, and along with the consideration that it would be an act of vandalism to

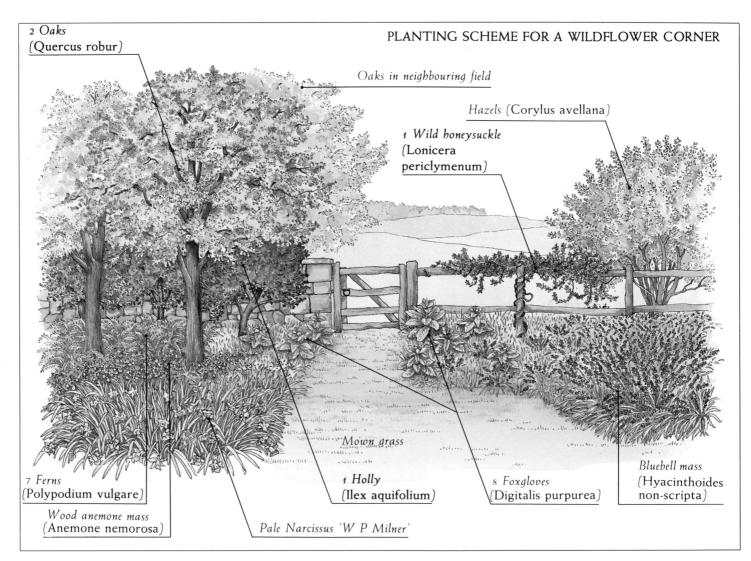

PLANTING SCHEME FOR A WILDFLOWER CORNER

2 Oaks
(Quercus robur)

Oaks in neighbouring field

Hazels (Corylus avellana)

1 Wild honeysuckle
(Lonicera periclymenum)

7 Ferns
(Polypodium vulgare)

Wood anemone mass
(Anemone nemorosa)

Pale Narcissus 'W P Milner'

Mown grass

1 Holly
(Ilex aquifolium)

8 Foxgloves
(Digitalis purpurea)

Bluebell mass
(Hyacinthoides non-scripta)

introduce alien wild species on any scale into a landscape environment with which it is not in accord. This sort of wildflower meadow may take up to three years to establish itself as the Monet'esque tapestry that you hold in your mind's eye.

A painfully tedious alternative to this method of establishing the wildflower meadow is to buy seedling wild species from a specialist nursery (or raise them yourself), which you grow on and plant out amongst established meadow grass. With maintenance these more mature specimens will be able to compete with the vigor of natives already growing there.

Grazed meadow look (right) *This kind of traditional grazed meadow look can be achieved by sowing mixed grasses with red clover* (Trifolium pratense), *daisies* (Bellis perennis) *and buttercups* (Ranunculus bulbosus) *mixed in with them.*

Flowery boundary (below) *In the lush, flowery period of late spring, encroaching wild flowers and grasses such as ragged Robin (here seen against foaming umbels of Queen Anne's Lace) can make a dramatic backdrop.*

FLOWERS FOR DRYING

There is an increasing interest in growing flowers that can be dried and used in arrangements for decoration. Many perennial flowers are suitable, some of which may be part of the country garden anyway. In this category are *Alchemilla vulgaris*, achillea, sedum heads, many of the thistles, and nearly all the grasses. Annuals may be grown, specially for drying (including grasses, strawflowers, cornflowers and marigolds) in broad swathes, amongst perennial masses in borders, or in the kitchen garden.

For the country dweller, the fields and hedgerows are a further source of plant material for drying—not just flowers, seedheads, cones, ferns and mosses, but also the stems of climbers such as wild clematis for twisting into wreaths, and twigs and branches for base material.

DRYING METHODS

There are a number of ways to dry plant material. The easiest, air drying, is simply a matter of hanging the flowers in small bunches with the heads down, in shaded, dry, airy conditions for a week or two, having first removed any leaves from the stems where they will touch in the binding. Or, if the stems are rigid enough, the flowers can be left to stand dry, in buckets or old bottles, arranged to allow air circulation between the stems and around the flower heads. Flowers such as delphiniums dry better after standing initially in a little water that you allow to evaporate.

Plants with textured leaves, that do not lend themselves to any of the other methods of drying, are traditionally preserved with a mixture of one part glycerine to two parts of hot water. The plant material becomes saturated with the glycerine, turning flowers and leaves a beige tone. Stems should be left to stand in the mixture, and large individual leaves should be immersed in it.

Poppy seedheads (right) *Poppy heads can be dried, attached to florist's wire and included in decorative arrangements, where they may be combined with acorns, nuts and pine cones.*

Hang drying (below) *In the summer, you can hang dry flowers (such as this lavender) outside, in an airy but shady spot.*

THE COTTAGE GARDEN

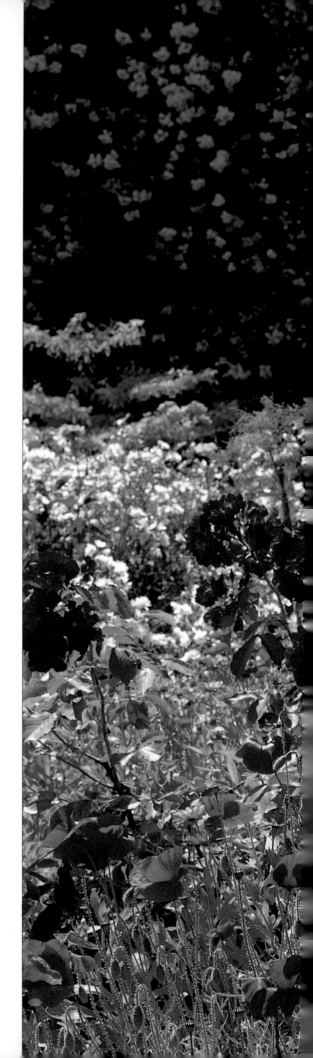

The popular image of the typical cottage gardener is of a gentle, white-haired old lady, bumbling through flowers, with a friendly cat rolling amongst carpets of pinks at her feet. Herbs hang from kitchen. beams or in the parlor ready to distil into homely remedies.

In fact, the dear old lady moved out ages ago. The new owners probably only weekend there with their two children and a retriever. These are the new country cottagers and where the old lady had an orchard which her husband scythed, Jacob's sheep now run free and their wool is woven at winter evening classes.

CHANGES OF USE

The cottage garden was once a place where a random mass of showy flowers and a vegetable patch represented brief respite from hard agricultural toil. Now its owners see the countryside that surrounds their cottage as charming and a place for relaxation, even if it is wholly agricultural. They are ecologically-minded, keen to preserve the character of their cottage and want a garden that suits their style.

They find, however, that what the local garden center peddles is not for them. Its merchandise is too urban and they want planting that complements the countryside around them as well as the building they have refurbished with care. The only requirement shared by traditional and new cottagers is that the garden look should still thrive on neglect so that precious hours spent at the cottage are not consumed in endless garden chores. It is also the low maintenance aspect that might encourage the country gardener in town to reproduce the new cottage style, although here the look will be contained.

The dream garden
(right) *Sun-kissed poppies against a backdrop of floribunda roses, with a white rambler tumbling through the hedgerow: the cottage gardener's idyll.*

Geraniums at the cottage window (left)
The classic cottage window-sill plants, geraniums (Pelargonium cvs.), are ideal for the weekender, since they require little care.

New cottage garden style still has much to do with the use of color. Sticking to a well defined plant color scheme is a sure way to make strong visual links both between the garden and the cottage, and the garden and the countryside beyond. Weatherboard (or clapboard) clad cottages will have a complementary stain or paint color. Clay-built or rendered elevations are traditionally color-washed. Brick and stone-built cottages have a wide but subtle range of wall tones to consider and, as with all cottages, have painted window frames and doorways, the colors of which must inspire your choice of plant color.

When thinking about harmony with colors outside your cottage garden, remember the changes of color with season, particularly how the color of maturing cereal crops can dominate countryside landscapes at a time when many country garden-style plants are at their peak.

INCLUDING A SURPRISE ELEMENT

An unexpected element has always been part of the essence of country garden style. The surprise element can be a sculptural incident (perhaps a piece of topiary if not true sculpture) that combines well with surrounding plant forms, or it might be the inclusion of vegetables and/or fruit amongst the predominantly decorative planting. What about including artichokes and the fennels, some asparagus perhaps, then in winter there are colored kales and the striking stems of kohl-rabi.

Herbs are very much part of the cottage garden scene under all sorts of guises and in multifarious leaf colours and shapes, since they are such good all-round garden plants. By these I mean rosemary, for instance, and lavender, and all the sages and thymes. Parsley makes a charming cottage garden edging plant.

GARDENING WITHOUT OBLIGATIONS

All these plants will add decorative as well as culinary value to the new cottage garden. And—since so many cottage owners are urban during the week—there is an added bonus and pleasure in being able to take vegetables and flowers back to town, without the obligation of a full scale vegetable garden.

For many the whole point of a cottage-type garden is its lack of obligation. The high-maintenance precedent set by picture book gardens and those "open to the public", is inhibiting rather than encouraging to those who have neither the time nor the inclination to maintain their garden to these standards.

The cottage garden gate (right) *Golden marjoram, sage and mints make up much of the planting that frames the classic picket gate to this traditional cottage garden.*

Cornish cottage garden (below left) *A profusion of herbs and grasses surrounds this Cornish cottage, linking it to the fields beyond its random hedge. The garden is alive with bees and butterflies.*

Fusing culinary interest with cottage tradition (below right) *This view shows part of the well-known vegetable garden at Barnsley House in Gloucestershire. Glorious vegetables in the foreground are mixed with lavender and standard rose bushes beyond.*

PLANNING A COTTAGE SCHEME

Once the builders move out, and the garden is secure from the incursions of surrounding livestock, the new cottage garden can start to take shape.

Begin by considering the color ranges that exist in your landscape through the seasons. Rugged hills and moorlands will give a background of muted browns, greens and mauves, while a predominantly agricultural countryside can produce a landscape of fresh greens and bright yellows in midsummer. Consider also the materials of your home, the color of the stone, slate and wood—particularly their color. Then start to select your plants, all the time imagining how they will look in maturity, once established against your cottage. Think of foliage as well as flower color, the plant's height after a fixed timescale of, say, five years, and the shape and general proportion of the plant.

PLANTING SCHEME FOR NEUTRAL WALLS

The cottage planting scheme, below, is planned to be seen against the traditional elevations of a south-of-England cottage, which has a weatherboarded upper story over buff-colored walls below. It would work well against any similarly neutral walls.

There is a strong skeleton of evergreen plants, including yews, viburnums, Choisya ternata *and the spectacular golden-leaved* Lonicera nitida 'Baggesen's Gold'. *This year-round plant material is a strong support for the more traditional perennial and annual cottage-style plants.*

1 Philadelphus lemoinei *'Erectus'*

3 Lonicera nitida *'Baggesen's Gold'*

1 *Whitebeam* (Sorbus aria *'Lutescens')*

6 *Foxgloves* (Digitalis grandiflora)

1 *Clematis montana 'Alba'*

1 *Lonicera halliana*

2 *Fastigiate yews* (Taxus bacatta *'Fastigiata')*

1 *Fasatigiate yew*

Shrub rose

7 *Santolina incana*

Marigold mass (Calendula officinalis)

1 *Mexican orange* (Choisya ternata)

5 *Lamb's ears* (Stachys lanata)

4 *Anemone japonica alba*

4 *Stinking hellebores* (Helleborus foetidus)

6 *Rudbeckia deamii*

3 *Viburnum tinus*

The two schemes below illustrate two different cottage planting schemes, each inspired by a specific cottage type. And since cottage types depend on local building traditions and materials, then the garden is guaranteed to complement the location too.

The scheme, below left, was designed for a traditional farm cottage in Sussex, in the south of England. It is constructed in brick with dark-stained weather boarding (or clapboard) across the first floor. The type has many permutations in the United Kingdom and United States. The planting creates the expected soft tumble of shrubby

and perennial plantings in a color scheme of brick-yellow with lemon and gray.

The scheme, below right, is styled for a north of England farmhouse with a fine stone barn adjacent to it. The house is a shade of green with old gold colored window surrounds, a combination that inspires the color scheme for the planting of pink and mauve with a creamy gold. The planting is designed to be seen both against the house and the beautiful Lakeland countryside that exists beyond this view, although it would also work, to an extent, in isolation in an enclosed garden.

SEMI-WILD SCHEME FOR COLORED WALLS

This planting plan has a strong color scheme of mauves and purples with yellow and white, planned to be seen against aquamarine color-washed walls—a traditional pigment. The scheme has a semi-natural feel since it includes native plants such as holly, ivy and gorse. The visual forms of giant hogweed and gorse are also strong enough to complement an adjoining stone barn.

2 Giant hogweed (Heracleum mantegazzianum)

1 English ivy (Hedera helix)

1 Holly (Ilex aquifolium)

12 Foxgolves (Digitalis purpurea)

1 Mallow (Malva sylvestris)

Self-seeded foxgloves

Chrysanthemum maximum *mass*

Valerian mass (Valeriana officinalis)

2 Rosa rubiginosa

3 Tree lupins (Lupinus arboreus)

3 Gorse (Ulex europaeus)

3 Flowering broom (Cytisus scoparius)

COTTAGE GARDEN PLANTS

Given the correct soil and aspect you can, of course, grow any plant in a cottage garden; but it is not any plant that will produce the effect shown opposite, with its relaxed charm, including the noble flower spikes of the Welsh onion (*Allium fistulosum*). Few of the latest hybrids with their gross double blooms and hectic colors suit. Softer perennial plant forms and flower colors should prevail over the bolder, architectural range of plants. Climbers have an important role, and there should be a range of winter flowers, along with masses of bulbs throughout the year. Lilies are a necessary ingredient, particularly the beautiful *Lilium candidum*, which always seems to be grown in rows in traditional cottage gardens. And roses too, in their climbing, rambling and shrub forms—standards, bush and hybrid teas are too sophisticated. Herbs, with some vegetables and fruit, make up the cottage garden palette.

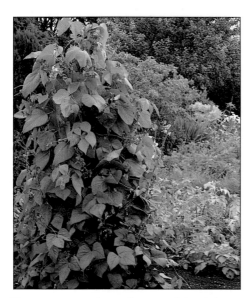

Decorative value of vegetables *Like many food plants, the runner bean is highly decorative in its own right.*

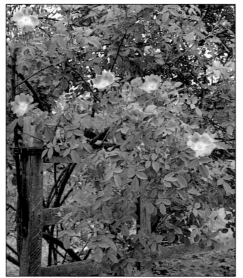

Shrub roses *A cottage garden would not be complete without shrub roses, in this case* Rosa canina 'Andersonii' *—a form of the dog briar.*

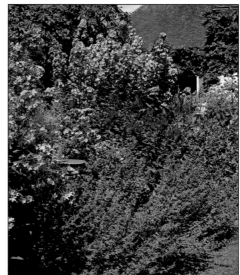

Massed perennials *Swathes of perennial veronica, ruby red asters and blue* Campanula lactiflora, *make the classic cottage look.*

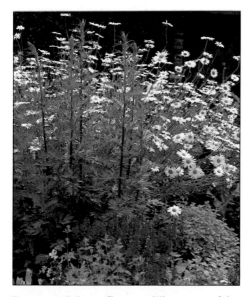

Perennial daisy flowers *The epitome of the cottage garden flower for full sun is the single form of* Chrysanthemum maximum.

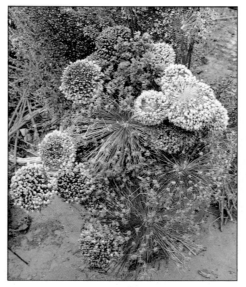

Bulbs Allium giganteum *(marvellous for dried flower arrangements) represents the bulbs that contribute to the cottage garden.*

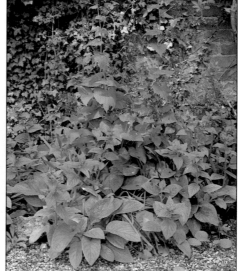

Honesty *Honesty* (Lunaria annua) *is a hardy garden biennial for light shade, shown here with* Omphalodes cappadocica.

ENCHANTED GARDEN

We have seen how, looking away from the house towards the boundary, the successful country garden welds itself into the surrounding countryside, while looking back to the house, the garden is styled to suit the building. But in the intervening zone (see p.28) it is possible to create yet another style that has to relate to neither, and this we might call the enchanted garden. It is often the part of a garden that fixes itself most strongly in the memory.

You do not necessarily need a large area to bring this idea to fruition, for while on the one hand it *could* be a walled garden, on the other the feeling of the enchanted garden can be evoked by a small visual incident that transports the imagination, sitting like a punctuation mark in the overall rhythm of the layout. Planting on its own is too transitory to fill the bill, while a seat, although useful for the enjoyment of the "otherness" of the enchanted garden, is too mundane. Some sculptural form is needed, what in the eighteenth century was termed an "eyecatcher".

COUNTRY GARDEN ORNAMENT

Most garden ornament is too grand by half, and it immediately looks pretentious placed in a modest layout. Classic sculpture is for classic layouts unless of course you use it with humor. Far better is a humbler feature — some beautifully constructed beehives perhaps, or a trophy of garden implements, or a simple piece of sculpture, not abstract, but a piece that makes a clear outline in concrete, stone or terracotta. Associated with the correct plant grouping, or contrasted with wildness, this combination contains more charm on the scale of the average garden than a dozen temples or urns.

Magic in the garden (right) *The happy abandonment of this faun gambolling in swathes of ramsons and wild parsley is very believable.*

Enchanting detail (left) *This frog spouting water forms part of a sculpture by Simon Verity, in the garden at Barnsley House, in the west of England.*

SCULPTURAL ORNAMENTS

The torso carved from fossilized rock (by Simon Verity) set amidst acanthus, opposite, represents a use of sculpture far removed from the placement of classical pieces in the garden. Once used to culminate a view molded by hedging or trees, this was considered the only accepted purpose of sculpture in the garden. In the country garden where the layout is more relaxed, such a use is now clearly inappropriate. Sculpture (and here I include any kind of informal sculptural ornament) is now more likely to be placed as a counterpoint to a fine tree or a good view, or as an interesting incident upon a terrace, for example. Alternatively, it can be positioned so as to create the centerpiece of its own enchanted world.

The forms of all the sculptural pieces below have a bold, simple outline, and properly sited they would add enormous interest to any garden.

Stone duck *This stone decoy duck sits in a bed of stonecrop and provides the sort of small incidental feature that brings a garden to life.*

Stone figure *The simple lines of this seated carved-stone figure are emphasized in silhouette against a green background.*

Discarded laundry mangle *An old white-painted mangle certainly provides a focal point of interest within the wild garden.*

  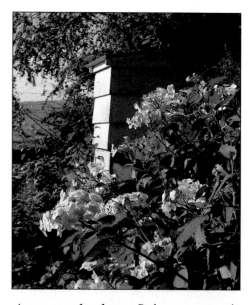

Fibreglass figure *This contemplative sculpture (by Marion Smith) sits overlooking water and bog plants.*

Concrete doves *These two doves (by Marie Gill) sit upon a simple brick plinth. The accompanying plant is* Fatshedera lizei.

Attractive beehives *Beehives can provide a simple, sculptural, but practical element. This one stands behind a hydrangea.*

FEATURES

For many, the absence of the "enchanted" element in their garden (and this applies to town as well as country gardens) is immediately remedied by adding yet another decorative element, another urn or a Gothic summer-house. All this does is to shore up the deficiency visually when in fact the flaw is probably a much more fundamental design problem. "Stuck-on" decoration is rarely the solution for a garden that lacks something magical; what is necessary is an eye-catching feature that is truly part of the garden layout. If it has sculptural qualities too, so much the better.

You might have been lucky enough to have inherited some splendid, eye-catching feature with the garden you moved to. A dovecot such as the one in the picture below is an example, or it might be some topiary or a formal pool. In such cases, your task will be to integrate the feature into the garden layout that *you* (and your family) require, and to assess the planting that accompanies it. Remember that there will probably be annual maintenance to undertake.

As far as new features for the country garden are concerned, I suggest an extension of the natural garden approach, using local materials to make a decorative but functional addition, perhaps along the lines of the stone jetty, below on the opposite page. Its harmony with the garden and its surroundings would be ensured by the use of local stone for the steps down and the causeway to the water's edge. Of course there are many other options. Seating is important in any garden and its provision might well inspire you to create a special feature—an arbor perhaps, or a lookout.

Special places to sit (right) *A simple seat or sitting area, might be all that is required to create an enchanted feel within a garden. The trunk-encircling seat, far right, commands a glorious view through iron railings, while engendering its own strong sense of place. The inviting beech tree arbor, right, has been lovingly trained against an iron frame.*

Grand dovecot (below) *This dovecot is certainly not a decorative afterthought; it embellishes a large building, over a shady loggia.*

STONE JETTY

*A small stone landing or jetty
with some steps down would combine with a
stream or garden pool, creating a place of quiet
repose where one might sit and dabble bare feet
in the cool water below on a summer's day.
This feature is for a stone area and should
utilize stone for its structure.*

Harmonious "natural" planting

Indigenous stone steps down

Indigenous stone causeway

*Natural stream
or informal man-made pool*

THE GARDEN IN SUMMER

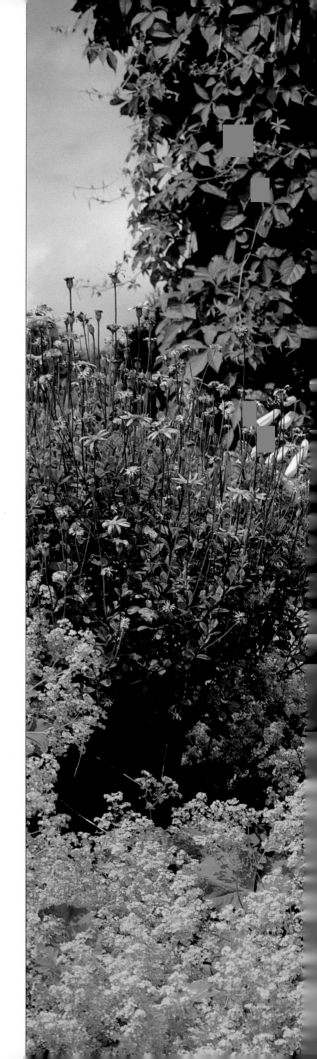

How selective memories of summer are. We usually only remember the pleasurable parts and these are invariably linked with the sun and fine weather—the times when you can sit outside for long lunches, or late into the evenings, bathed with a heady scent of honeysuckle, tobacco plants and lilies. The summertime garden is a totally sensuous experience, its scents and sounds combining to frame the joy of summer living. Now is the time to sunbathe, to potter, to pick and generally enjoy the fruits of your springtime labors, while tolerating the chores of grass cutting and watering in the cool stillness of the evening.

Rose blooms surely herald early summer and the increasing fullness of the garden, but it is not a particularly flowery time of the year among native plants since the first flush of blooms is over with spring. There are, however, musky scented phlox, daisies and dahlias if you have a liking for them. It's the countryside beyond that is the most memorable thing about high summer—golden corn and stubble, picnics, and that peculiarly dull heaviness of surrounding tree foliage as it loses its spring freshness and creates deep pools of shadow.

There is a blanched look about the landscape if it has been hot and dry and flower colors have certainly strengthened, building to what will be their autumnal crescendo. Given moisture, gardens look full blown and things that have a mind to self-seed will have done so. Grasses are long and lush, and climbers rampant. Lushness describes much of the summer mood, and we live our lives outdoors in its full fruiting flood. Ponds, lakes and streams become irresistible attractions. Finally, the vigorous growth of the garden will need to be controlled and cut back in anticipation of the autumn tidy-up to come.

A fragrance of summer (right) *The perfume of lilies can be almost over-powering. Here they have been grown in pots for easy moving. The blue kingfisher daisy (*Felicia *sp.) is a half-hardy annual.*

A sound of summer (left) *The buzzing of bees is particularly evocative of summer. They love thistle heads, in this case* **Eryngium giganteum** *'Miss Wilmott's Ghost'.*

SUMMER FRUITS

The soft and pitted fruits of summer can be a glorious bonus for the country gardener,
from the earliest gooseberries—tough and reliable—to the treasured crops of
sun-ripened strawberries. Some fruits, such as cherries, are an incidental bonus,
whereas the berries are plants for the fruit garden and require special husbandry.
Early, middle and late varieties spread the season to your requirements.

Blueberry
(Vaccinium corymbosum)
*The bush thrives in acid,
damp soil, and has attractive flowers and leaf color*

Gooseberries for cooking
(Ribes uva-crispa *var.*)
*When half-ripened, the fruits
can be sour*

Blackcurrant
(Ribes nigrum)
*Bushes require warmth
and protection*

Gooseberries for dessert (Ribes uva-crispa *var.*)
Fully ripe fruits are very sweet

Red currant
(Ribes sativum)
*Require similar conditions
to gooseberries but with
a sheltered site*

Tay berry
(Rubus idaeus × fruticosus)
A prolific cross between blackberry and raspberry

Raspberry
(Rubus idaeus *var.*)
For the sunniest situation in the fruit garden and traditionally grown on wires

Wild strawberry
(Fragaria vesca)
The little plants make a decorative addition—their fruit has great flavor

Strawberry
(Fragaria *hybrids*)
Essential for summer desserts, strawberries require a well-drained patch in the fruit garden

Sweet cherry
(Prunus avium)
(two varieties)
Different varieties must bloom together for a usable crop

ENJOYING THE SUNSHINE

Much of the joy of a country garden in summer is associated with sitting, eating and drinking in it. The vagaries of summer weather in many climes, however, along with morning and evening dews, often make the *fête champêtre*, a picnic on the ground, impossible. The answer is some form of seating which can be relaxed in, left out at night, and is tough enough for children to turn into an assault course. It is important too that seating is a feature in its own right, not a dominant one, but a feature none the less that harmonizes with its location.

The ideal country garden furniture is probably not painted white, is not metal and is certainly not smart. The chances are it is made of wood, which looks the part and is tough enough for the job. There are all kinds of wooden furniture that you can buy, while there is always the option of designing, and even constructing, your own, remembering that a relaxing seat is one that is generous and sturdy.

SIMPLE FURNITURE

My preference is for very simple wooden benches. Facsimiles of Sir Edwin Lutyens's celebrated bench designs are now easily obtainable, constructed in teak, oak, or cedar. The chairs and tables to match are similarly solid, comfortable and secure, but far from cheap. For many rural situations there is absolutely nothing wrong with re-using simple wooden kitchen chairs and a solid pine table, although treated with preservative. Close to the house these will be far more in character than the smartest "patio ensemble".

Half barrels (the coopered sort) of various sizes with bright splashes of annual color growing in them look particularly good with timber furniture close to buildings. Choose a complementary color scheme for your annuals in tubs and stick to it—the visual result will be much stronger than if you allow an ill-assorted color mix.

Another visual delight, and enjoyable too, is the hammock. Slung between gnarled apple trees, its lazy presence is the confirmation of hot, high-summer days.

A summer's feast (right) *Blueberries and blue vein cheese— ingredients for a summer lunchtime feast. Such delights look all the better against* Clematis *'Vyvyan Pennell'.*

Shaded bench seat (below left) *A wooden bench and planted half- barrels look perfect in the country garden. The timber should be brushed down to remove mildew, and restained with preservative once a year.*

The potting table (below) *When the greenhouse becomes unbearably hot, an outdoor table for potting is a useful piece of furniture for a working corner of the garden.*

SALAD CROPS

Any country garden in summer can produce salad ingredients
of high quality to titillate the palate with their crisp freshness.
The decorative qualities of the growing plants are an
undoubted bonus.

Coriander (Coriandrum sativum)
*Use sparingly in strong-flavored,
midsummer salads*

Chives (Allium
schoenoprasum)
*Adds a refreshingly
tangy bite to any salad*

Tomato (Lycopersicon
lycopersicum) *Small, sweet,
and full of health-giving vitamins*

Spring onion (Allium cepa)
*Picked young and tender for
both the bulb and leaves*

Fennel (Foeniculum
vulgare) *Striking aniseed-
flavored plant*

Baby zucchini
(Cucurbita pepo)
*Eaten when the fruit
is still unripe, after
removing the corolla*

Radish (Raphanus sativus)
*Refreshing, crisp mouthfuls;
plants require plenty of moisture
during growth*

Globe artichoke
(Cynara scolymus)
*A delectable vegetable
from a handsome plant*

Corn salad (Valerianella locusta) *A small plant, but producing a useful quantity of leaves*

Oak-leaved lettuce (Lactuca sativa) *One of the attractive, crispy forms of leaf lettuce*

Radicchio (Cichorium intybus) *Has a similar tasty bitterness to chicory*

Endive (Cichorium endivia) *Has a stronger flavor than lettuce and is more hardy*

Asparagus (Asparagus officinalis) *Fleshy and tender spears, cut below ground level as they sprout above it*

Red-leaved lettuce (Lactuca sativa) *Crisp, curly-leaved variety with striking dark-red edging*

THE NEW BORDER

While a herbaceous perennial border can look superb, the work it demands is enormous considering how short a period it looks its best. Incorporating woody plant material (and herbs and annuals) into the arrangement will give it much added interest and, if they are evergreen, extend the interest into other seasons as well. Include the odd climber on the fence or wall behind too and you will loosen up the regimented form of the border enormously and give it a more natural look.

Controlling the number of species in the new border, leaving room for bigger masses of what you do include, will make the effect as dramatic as possible. Your efforts will fail visually, however, unless the border is deep enough. If you intend including woody material anything under 2 m (6 ft) wide is too thin.

One of the characteristic features of such a mixed border is that it should appear to be so full that the material is overflowing. If the border abuts a lawn, it is best to lay a hard edging (brick or paving slabs) a fraction below the level of the lawn so that the bed can ooze on to that and not impede the mowing process. It is better still if your mixed planting abuts a gravel area, since you can plant some of the foreground species into the gravel itself (see p. 107) to extend the ooze. Small foreground stachys (that is the non-flowering variety *Stachys lanata* 'Silver Carpet'), feverfew and iris are good for this. Ideal smaller plants still include bugle (*Ajuga spp*), and varieties of *Allium*.

Effective use of strong summer colors (right) *In this mixed border, the strong summer yellows of achillea and verbascum, and reds of dahlias and nasturtiums, have maximum effect against a background of abundant green.*

When is a border a border? (below) *The hydrangea, rosemary and alchemilla grouping (left), and that of hebe, rheum and feverfew beneath an apricot (right), are both far from traditional summer borders, as they include sculptural form and bold masses.*

DAISY FLOWERS

Daisy-like blooms are, generally speaking, a pleasure of high and late summer in the country garden. They are mostly the flowers of herbaceous perennials, the main type of plant in the traditional herbaceous border, particularly species and cultivars of the genus *Chrysanthemum*.

China aster (Callistephus chinensis) *The double-flowered form of this slightly tender annual*

Marguerites (Chrysanthemum frutescens) *Yellow- or white-flowering perennial, grown as an annual in colder climates*

Chrysanthemum × morifolium *'Snapper' Single type flower*

Chrysanthemum × morifolium
'Penny Lane' Single type flower

Chrysanthemum indicum *Spoon type flower*

September flower (Chrysanthemum sp.) *Produces a mass of tiny flowerheads in late summer*

Chrysanthemum × morifolium *'Carra' (right) Single type flower*

Immortelle (Xeranthemum annuum) *An annual with flowers that will dry well for winter decoration*

Chrysanthemum × morifolium *'Statesman' A mini pompon type*

Feverfew (Chrysanthemum parthenium) *Hardy perennial species that self-seeds freely*

Chrysanthemum × morifolium *'Rejour' (left) Single type flower*

China aster (Callistephus chinensis) *Semi-double form*

SUMMER COLOR

It is a sad fact that much native flower color will have spent itself by summer. Only in the perennial garden can you hope to sustain any sort of show, and even that is difficult in high summer if the planting is truly mixed and you are striving, in a limited area, to maintain a color scheme. Planning for a display in a border devoted completely to high summer and autumn blooms is an easier matter, but interweaving flower interest for different seasons can be awkward. Particular plants are a great help, however, such as the sweetly-scented *Hosta plantaginea*, which retains its fresh green foliage when other hostas look tired, and produces white trumpet flowers very late in summer. A comparatively new variety of hosta called 'Honeybells' is related to it.

In the great traditional gardens of the early part of the century, the problem was overcome by either sinking pots of plants of particular interest for a period and then replacing them (using many gardeners) or interplanting perennials with annuals. The latter method is a useful technique for the modern country garden. A favorite of mine for this infill job is the tall white nicotiana, which smells so good at night. Its green cousin is also excellent.

Cool swathes of color (right) *Massed delphiniums with* Rosa rubrifolia *form a backdrop to white* Aster *sp. with yellow* Lysimachia *sp. and* Centaurea *sp. in this display of cool summer colors.*

High summer flowers for decoration (below) *Larkspur, delphiniums, white helipterum and amaranthus can all be dried.*

OLD-FASHIONED ROSES

Unlike most modern roses, bred solely for showy blooms, old, shrub and some climbing roses, are hardy, low-maintenance shrubs with a host of visual attributes.

Rosa filipes 'Kiftsgate' (left)
Delicate, clustered blooms belie a rambling rose of great vigor

Chapeau de Napoleon
A centifolia rose

Ferdinand Pichard
A hybrid perpetual with striped globular blooms

James Mitchell (below)
Attractive "mossed" seedheads of this small-flowered, magenta-pink moss rose

Baby Fauras
Tiny polyantha rose, to 30cm (12in)

Gertrude Jekyll (above)
A new rose with rosette blooms and strong old rose fragrance

Souvenir du Dr Jamain (left)
A hybrid perpetual with double, deep cup blooms

The Portland Rose
A Damask rose, making a small bush

Rosa sericea pteracantha
A variety noted for its huge translucent thorns amongst ferny foliage

Zéphirine Drouhin (left)
*A Bourbon climbing rose
of exceptional fragrance*

**Rosa macrophylla
'Master Hugh'**
*Naturally occurring form with
some of the largest hips*

Louise Odier
*Exquisite Bourbon
rose with strong perfume
and bushy habit*

Blush Noisette
*An old climbing rose
of the noisette type,
for a warm wall*

Madame Isaac Pereire
*A tall, vigorously growing
Bourbon rose of great fragrance —
can be used as a climber*

Baroness Rothschild
*A hybrid perpetual rose,
with richly-scented, saucer
blooms in dense foliage*

The Fairy
*A polyantha rose, but its
habit is larger than the normal,
growing to a meter (3ft) high*

Gloire de Dijon
*This rose is a cottage garden
favorite of the noisette class,
with open-cupped blooms*

SUMMER TASKS

Summer is not just for relaxing outside. What seemed pristine at the end of spring quite quickly begins to look tired, and the spring-flowering species need cutting back to encourage a possible flowering in autumn. Climbers need to be tied in or back as they grow; many of those seemingly casual arrangements of clematis clambering through this or that do in fact need some thought and manipulation from time to time. These are creative tasks that take but a minute of your time as you saunter in the garden.

But much of summer's labor is simply the mowing. The new country gardener is not troubled by the daily attentions involved in producing a lawn tennis court finish. But in a summer of some sun, some rain, where grass is the chief groundcover, mowing becomes a weekly chore, which has its rewards in the glorious smell of new-mown grass and the crisper look of the sward compared with the burgeoning growth elsewhere. By including areas of rough grass in the layout, which need cutting less often, some of the work can be reduced.

Watering may become another chore. The watering of newly-planted specimens may well start as early as mid-spring whenever there is a prolonged dry spell. Light, gravelly or sandy soils can dry out for months at a time in mid-summer, when a good soaking once a week will prolong the freshness of a garden enormously.

Creative lawn mowing (opposite) *This is an early summer display of dog daisies in rough grass on either side of a mown path. Such a lawn takes up to three years to establish from scratch.*

The ever-present garden hose (below) *The device seen against the white froth of Crambe cordifolia flowers is a sensible tidying post for the indispensible summertime equipment, the garden hose.*

GRASSES

There is infinitely more to grass in the country garden than a mown lawn. This selection of elegant stems, leaves and seedheads was taken from my garden in mid-summer and displays discreet qualities of shape, texture and color. All these specimens are easy to grow and most are tolerant of indifferent soil.

Sedge (Carex morrowii *'Variegata'*)
Ideally suited to a partly-shaded pool margin

Purple moor-grass (Molina caerulea *'Variegata'*), right.
Tuft-forming perennial

Zebra-striped rush (Miscanthus sinensis *'Zebrinus'*)
Attractive lateral stripes

Fescue (*Festuca ovina glauca*), below

Creeping soft grass (Holcus mollis), above.
Variegated form of a perennial, acid-loving grass

New Zealand sedge (Uncinia unciniata) *A visually-striking, dark brown species*

Sedge (Carex stricta *'Bowles' Golden'*) *Golden yellow form of this tender, moisture-loving perennial*

Feather grass
(Stipa 'Variegata')
*A meter-high (3-ft) form
whose flower-
heads glisten purple
on opening*

Feather grass (Stipa arundinaria)
*Prefers a dry and sunny position
and is useful in arrangements*

Lyme grass (Elymus
arenarius), right.
*Vigorous in most soils
although native of
sandy habitats*

THE WATER GARDEN

In the mind's eye, the perfect country garden has a natural stream coursing through its site, or has a pond with rushes, lily pads and ducks, to coincide with the lowest part of the garden where the water table naturally surfaces. But what of the majority of us whose gardens are not blessed with such idyllic features? Must we forego the inimitable sights and sounds of water and the undoubted contribution its presence makes in the country garden in terms of attracting wildlife of all sorts?

The answer, thankfully, is no, as long as your garden is not in a location where water would never establish itself naturally, such as a hill top. You can introduce water artificially, but its artificiality should not be apparent in the country garden. It is not the place for formal pools but rather for features that are, in some form or another, credible interpretations of naturally-occurring water.

PRACTICALITIES

It is tempting to try to reproduce the excitement of fast-moving natural water in the garden, a brook chattering over rocks with pools and eddies, or the languid, serpentine sweep of a lowland stream. Such a feature is extremely difficult to falsify on anything but a small scale, and requires resources and effort that contradict the relaxed, natural approach that the new country garden epitomizes. An informal area of still water, along the lines of the pool shown on page 157, is far more practical a proposition. Such a feature is so visually attractive that its presence will create the feel of the enchanted garden and it might therefore be sited in the intermediate zone of the garden (see p. 126), although the foremost requirement is a naturalistic site in a hollow.

Man-made but marvellous (right) *A natural-looking pool, such as this with its lilies, reeds, rushes, hemerocallis and eryngium, creates a feeling of instant tranquility.*

Natural water course (left) *A fast-moving stream in your garden is an all dominating feature that requires little gilding. Here ferns and iris are enough.*

NATURAL WATER

Should you be in the enviable position of having natural water within, running through, bordering or adjoining your garden, it will be very difficult to resist the temptation to garden its edges in a decorative way and generally "to make the most of it". Such a step can be a mistake, for, on the one hand, the natural beauty of the stream or pond will emphasize the man-made feel of the additions, and, on the other, the alien decoration will take the edge off the natural charm of the original. Nevertheless, you have a feature and want to exploit it.

The first step is to establish the essential character of the stream. Is it rocky and fast or mud-lined and sluggish? Notice how the force of water sculpts its containment, cutting into the bank on the outside of bends and leaving a beach on the inside. What about the nature of that beach—are its pebbles round or flat? The tallest planting

will be at the back, getting smaller to the front of the newly established, dryer ground. You can extend and dramatize this natural look by planting in bold, simple groups and using strong plant form and leaf contrast.

Against this simple setting you might go on to introduce man-made features, the most obvious being the bridge. Keep the shape simple—there is no need for the Gothic nor Japanese styles when it comes to the basic form and/or the decoration of a bridge.

Chalk stream (right) *In chalk country, streams brim to the banks of their daisy-sprinkled banks. The rampant white rose 'Kiftsgate' strikes just the right level of decorative gardening in this example.*

Rocky-bedded stream (below) *In hard rock regions, streams rush along narrow, boulder-strewn courses making turns that create little beaches of pebbles. Their natural beauty needs no guilding.*

WATER FEATURES

Whereas in a town garden you might introduce the sound of running water perfectly adequately (trickling from a pipe through a wall, for example) using a modest electrical pump and a small cistern, the country equivalent of such a feature is on a much larger scale—the waterfall associated with a mill-pond, or the high drama of a natural waterfall. It is even possible (but difficult), in the self-contained world of a town garden, to re-create a section of a tiny brook, trickling over and through rocks; but how insignificant and inappropriate this would be in the country.

BUILDING A POOL

There is, however, a viable country-scale equivalent to the formal town garden pool, and that is a feature such as the natural-style pool shown in the plan below. It is a compromise between the completely wild pond and a cultivated garden pool, with approximately half of its perimeter retained by a low brick wall, while the remainder consists of earth bank or cobble beach. A mechanical excavator is needed for a pool of such dimensions (27.5 m (90ft) long by 1.5 m (5 ft) deep in its center) before lining with sand and a heavy-gauge black, butyl-rubber liner. The retaining wall should be built on top of the liner. Some of the excavated earth can be pushed down into the pool (over the liner) and shaped to create a muddy area. The planting in this mud and on the bank behind, combined with the cobble beach and the sheet of still water itself, makes a strong feature.

Country scale (right) *The overflow from a mill-pond over a robust stone retaining wall is now a purely decorative element in this garden. It is of a large enough scale to provide a powerfully attractive water feature.*

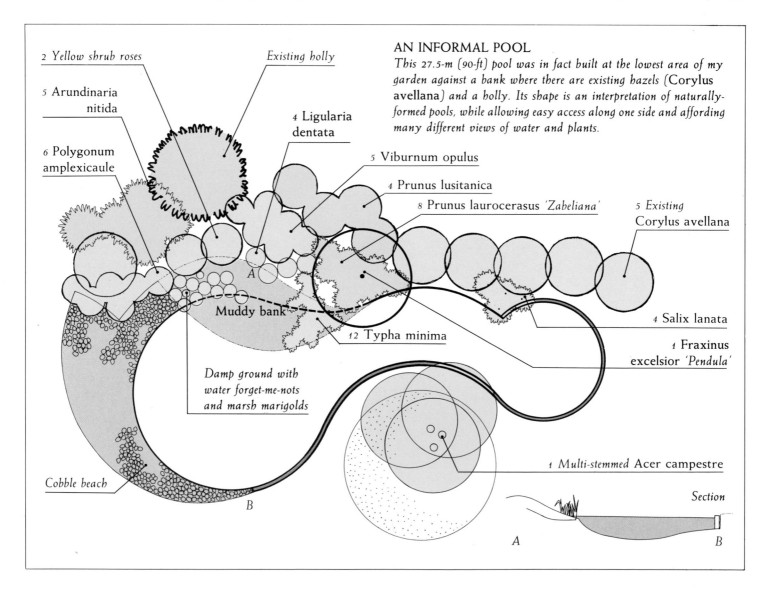

2 Yellow shrub roses

5 Arundinaria nitida

6 Polygonum amplexicaule

Existing holly

4 Ligularia dentata

AN INFORMAL POOL

This 27.5-m (90-ft) pool was in fact built at the lowest area of my garden against a bank where there are existing hazels (Corylus avellana) and a holly. Its shape is an interpretation of naturally-formed pools, while allowing easy access along one side and affording many different views of water and plants.

5 Viburnum opulus

4 Prunus lusitanica

8 Prunus laurocerasus 'Zabeliana'

5 Existing Corylus avellana

A

Muddy bank

12 Typha minima

Damp ground with water forget-me-nots and marsh marigolds

4 Salix lanata

1 Fraxinus excelsior 'Pendula'

1 Multi-stemmed Acer campestre

Cobble beach

B

A

Section

B

WATER PLANTING

The attraction of a mixed-planting group in association with water is due to the combination of strong leaf forms (often vertical) with the horizontal line of water itself. The added attractions of some color and some insect life bring great potential for a marvellous addition to the country garden.

While most bog and waterside plants will flourish and are easy enough to care for once established, they have, in the main, very specific moisture requirements—some take any moist soil while others need to stand in up to 15 cm (6 in) of water. A great disadvantage is that few are evergreen, so the pond-side can look very bare in winter. Flowering tends to be from spring until early summer, after which the pond-side can look spent and drab. The secret therefore is to extend the period of interest over as long a summer time-span as possible through careful selection of water-loving plants.

Some of the earliest water plants to flower are the marsh-marigolds (*Caltha palustris*) with water forget-me-nots (*Myosotis* sp.). Then come the flag iris (*Iris pseudoacorus*), followed by the early summer-flowering Japanese water iris (*Iris laevigata*). The wide range of primulas take over until, by late summer, the reeds and rushes (*Typha* spp.) produce their characteristic dark rounded poker flowers.

Water lilies will flower right through the period, until they are caught by the first frosts.

To sustain a natural look, waterside planting should not appear like a perennial flower border. Most natural waterside planting tends to consist of a single type of plant growing in a bold mass.

There is also a range of perennials and woody shrubs that look well growing in association with water, although this is not necessarily their original habitat. I am particularly fond of the shrubby willows and dogwoods (see pp.58-59)—their colored stems are marvellous for winter interest.

Arum lily (right) *The white spathes of the arum lily (*Zantedeschia aethiopica*) show up well against the enormous leaves of* Gunnera manicata. *The foreground plants growing in the water are arrowheads (*Sagittaria *sp.), whose foliage is indispensable for a natural planting.*

Flags and loosestrife (below left) *The white flag (*Iris pseudacorus alba*), yellow loosestrife (*Lysimachia punctata*) and, on the left,* Rodgersia *sp. make this lovely and colorful plant combination for a pool-side situation.*

Early flowering marsh marigold (below) *The single yellow marsh marigold (*Caltha palustris*) is one of the earliest flowering aquatic plants. There are other forms of it, including double and white.*

THE SHADE GARDEN

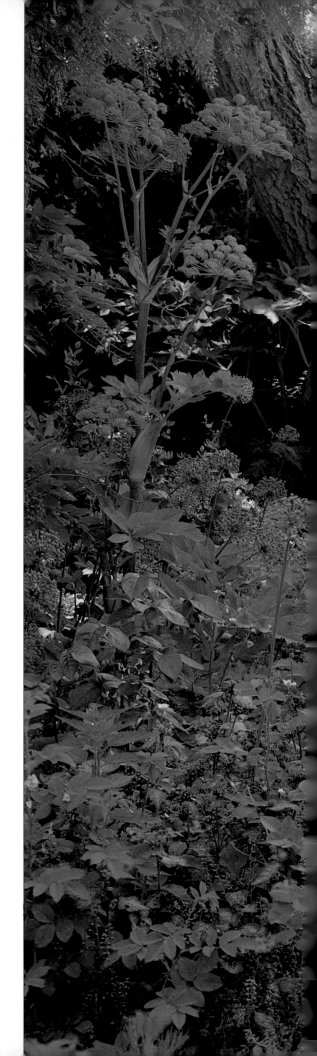

While in many countries summer shade is a prized commodity, through-out much of the gardened world people bemoan it, saying that little will grow there. And being discouraged by shade is an urban complaint as well as a rural one. It is true that there are a few forest trees beneath which little will grow—beeches, horse chestnuts and mature conifers in particular—but the shade of which gardeners complain is more often that cast by a building or a wall, or the dappled shade caused by trees and shrubs of lesser size. The density of shade caused by tree foliage can be altered by thinning their heads, changing deep shade to medium or medium to light. Thinning is quite different to cutting back, since the aim is to *retain* the overall size of the tree but to reduce its thickness. This you achieve by removing selected boughs in winter, when the tree's sap is low (it is advisable to have a tree surgeon under-take the work). Light shade can be turned to advantage simply by choosing from the many plants that thrive in shady conditions.

SHADE-TOLERANT PLANTS

Many of the plants that enjoy shade have gradually adapted themselves to life in reduced light by developing large leaves. Visually, this characteristic makes them very attractive material to plant; the many forms of hosta are a fine example. The flower color of shade-loving specimens tends to be pale, however.

There is also a whole range of ground-covering plants that is excellent for semi-shade conditions, plants such as *Vinca* sp. or *Rubus tricolor*, which will even become too rampant. So far from being a disadvantage, a shaded area can become very attractive.

Semi-shaded glory
(right) Alchemilla
vulgaris, *with* Polygonum
and Angelica *spp. make up
the perennial ground-cover
of this semi-shaded area.*

Autumnal shade (left)
Cyclamen neapolitanum
*will form a dainty carpet.
The marbling of the leaves is
as attractive a feature as
the flowers themselves.*

SHADE PLANTING

Shade with moisture provides ideal growing conditions for many plants, dappled shade being the best. As long as your soil is not alkaline, such conditions provide the natural habitat for all the rhododendrons and azaleas and also camellias and maples. The plants for shade with a chalky soil are fewer, but *Aucuba japonica* (a much maligned plant) and its relative *Prunus laurocerasus*, the laurel, with many of the viburnums, will do well in such conditions.

Smaller shrubs for shade and most soil types belong to the genera *Rhus, Elaeagnus, Hamamelis, Helleborus* and *Hydrangea*. The elders (*Sambucus* spp.) are excellent, quick-growing shrubs for the semi-wild look. The range

Water cistern feature (right) *The gentle lady fern (Athyrium filix-femina) makes an attractive incident on the shady side of a decorative water cistern.*

Flower color for shade (opposite) *The orange lily flowers of Crocosmia sp., against the deep green of ferns, make a dramatic counterpoint to naturalized, blue-flowering hydrangeas in damp, acid soil.*

Solomon's seal (below) *Solomon's seal (Polygonatum multiflorum) has both attractive arching branches of foliage and cream-scented flowers in spring hanging from the axils.*

includes variegated and cut-leaf forms that have great charm. For groundcover *Vinca* spp. are excellent — *Vinca minor* being a tidier and hardier plant than *Vinca major*.

PLANTS FOR DRY SHADE

The dry shaded area is rather more difficult to cope with horticulturally than is the damp shaded one. Dry shade is usually found in association with buildings, where the soil is often clay because of its suitability as a base for foundations.

Bamboos (*Arundinaria* spp.) are excellent in this situation, but they do not like wind. The *Berberis* genus, along with mahonias and cotoneasters, are great stand-bys. Species of *Skimmia* are also shrubs that tolerate dry shade and make excellent components for the framework of a planting scheme. For groundcover use ajuga (which is good in dry and damp shade), bergenia and euonymous.

Shaded waterside site (right) *Growing in the shade of both a Japanese and a field maple, is a mass of scaly male ferns* (Dryopteris pseudomas). *The pale points of color are wild balsam and a low, cream-flowering* Hydrangea quercifolia.

White anemones (below) *The white-flowering Japanese anemone* (Anemone × hybrida 'Alba') *is a captivating plant, providing late summer interest in light shade.*

THE WORKING GARDEN

The only sort of country garden for many is the working garden. These people enjoy the satisfaction of producing fresh fruit and vegetables and the noble act of cultivation that goes with it. They may even be tempted by the wholesome advantages of self-sufficiency.

However, many of us now find that just as our cherished crops are ready for picking, so are those at the local "pick-your-own". So the new working garden might be put to better use by growing a more limited but special range of vegetables and fruit. A range perhaps inspired by culinary requirements, including crops that are always a treat to the palate, such as asparagus tips or globe artichokes.

THE SOIL

With purely decorative gardening you can turn the nature of your site and soil to advantage, choosing a style and range of plants that complement it, whether it be exposed and sandy or shaded and damp. However, the nature of the soil, how much there is of it, and whether or not it receives plenty of growth-inducing sunshine, are decisive factors when it comes to the working garden.

A light sandy soil is the easiest, since it warms up and dries out quickly in spring and is relatively easy to work. But its open, fast-draining texture means it will require regular feedings or it will lose its fertility rapidly. The chalky soils that occur over gravel have a "sweetness" (alkalinity) that produces good vegetables. Heavy clay soils are cold and difficult to break up, since they dry out so late after winter. When well-fed and conditioned, they will nevertheless produce excellent crops.

Healthy beauty (right)
The celebrated vegetable garden at Barnsley House, in Gloucestershire, has all the wholesome ingredients of the working garden combined with obvious charm.

Food with good looks
(left) *The wide range of attractive cabbage forms includes slow-growing, crinkly savoys, and varieties of the common cabbage with pink-tinged veins.*

USING FOOD CROPS DECORATIVELY

The dramatic planting in the beautiful, church-side garden below, is solely of culinary crops. Crispy-leaved parsley grows in front of the majestic foliage of globe artichokes, which, in turn give way to an explosion of feathery asparagus. More and more, gardeners are recognizing the visual attributes of vegetables and fruit, and including them in general mixed plantings of shrubs and perennials.

This is increasingly done in smaller gardens, where there is not enough space for a separate kitchen garden.

The idea is not so novel when you consider the now well-established decorative uses of culinary herbs. To these you can add corn, ornamental cabbages (for wonderful autumn color and form) and species of the genus *Rubus* (blackberry) purely for their looks.

Blackcurrant *Not quite so spectacular as its redcurrant cousin, blackcurrants are still a useful addition to any fruit garden.*

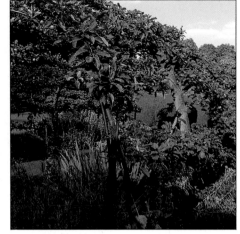

Trained fruit *Fruit trees trained over a path create a fascinating tunnel effect whether bare-stemmed, in flower, or in fruit.*

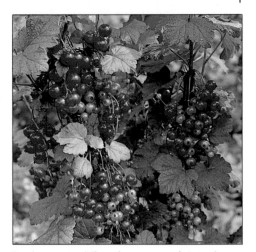

Redcurrant *Though an insignificant plant for much of the year, the redcurrant in fruit provides a bright splash of summer color.*

Lettuce varieties *Rank upon rank of different lettuce varieties produces a subtle blend of visual and tactile effects.*

Onions *Rows of onions prior to their harvesting at the end of summer make an interesting abstract pattern on the ground.*

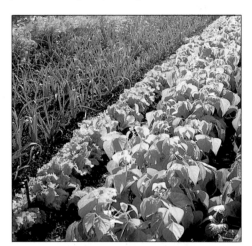

Light greens *Not a flower in sight, but the quality of light reflected by the leaves of bush beans, lettuce and leeks is stunning.*

Florence fennel *The extraordinary fan-shaped bulbous stems of Florence fennel are topped with typical fern-like foliage.*

Winter cabbage *There is a vast range of plants in the brassica genus, none more sumptuous than the good old winter cabbage.*

Ruby chard *The scarlet stems of ruby chard provide spectacular late summer color when massed within a mixed planting.*

LIVESTOCK

For those with a garden too large to manage, the idea of keeping some sheep, a donkey or some geese to keep the grass down can sound like a simple answer. But it is all too easy to swop one set of gardening problems for another of the two or four-legged kind. Any livestock needs containment, supervision and management, so it is probably best to seek the co-operation of a friendly farmer to see if he will put his animals on your land. He might be pleased for a little extra grazing for some sheep, for example. Of course you must make sure that your fencing is adequate to keep the animals from straying on to roads, but the responsibility for the stock remains the farmer's.

There are many parents who have given way to their children's request for a pony, thereby involving themselves in a great responsibility, not only to the poor animal but to the community at large. The semi-suburban areas on the perimeter of most large towns now have acres of dissipated substandard grazing, ill-fenced, mismanaged and cluttered with unsound structures in which unfortunate animals survive, often loved, but in fact neglected through ignorance.

However, there are others who are interested in and concerned about their stock, many of whom are doing valuable work in saving rare breeds of domestic cattle, pigs, sheep and fowl. Such animals do not have a direct commerical value nowadays, but their unique genetic patterns are a valuable resource that deserves saving.

Half the point of keeping livestock is to see and enjoy it, so some manipulation of fencing boundaries, or removal of shrubbery, may be necessary to bring shelters and runs into the overall garden concept. It may be seen against the backdrop of surrounding landscape (and even be an extension of its mood) or it might somehow be incorporated into the transitional zone of the garden layout (see Zone B on p.28).

Any sort of livestock is a huge responsibility on a number of levels and its maintenance should not be considered lightly.

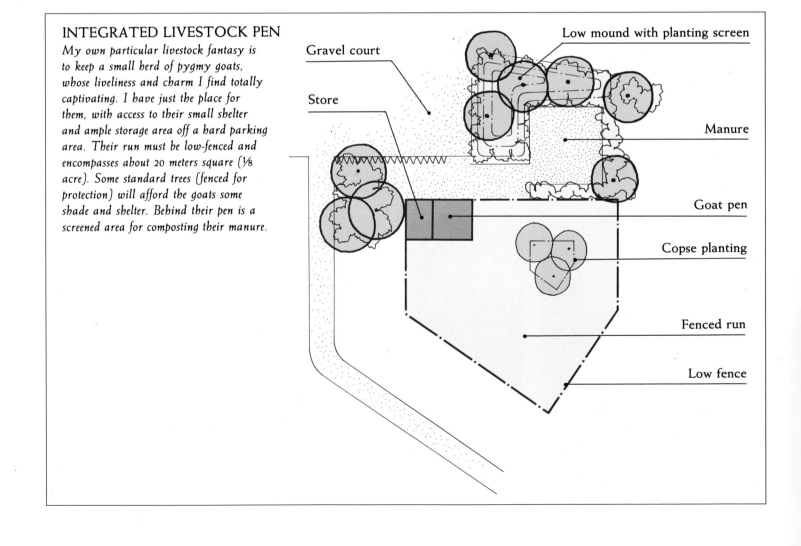

INTEGRATED LIVESTOCK PEN

My own particular livestock fantasy is to keep a small herd of pygmy goats, whose liveliness and charm I find totally captivating. I have just the place for them, with access to their small shelter and ample storage area off a hard parking area. Their run must be low-fenced and encompasses about 20 meters square (⅛ acre). Some standard trees (fenced for protection) will afford the goats some shade and shelter. Behind their pen is a screened area for composting their manure.

Gravel court

Store

Low mound with planting screen

Manure

Goat pen

Copse planting

Fenced run

Low fence

Goats *All goats have great character, but they need permanent weatherproof shelter and supervision since they should not be left outside in cold conditions, in the rain or overnight.*

Ducks *Not only are ducks such as these Buff Orpingtons the perfect visual complement to a pond or stream, but they also provide eggs and meat for the kitchen table.*

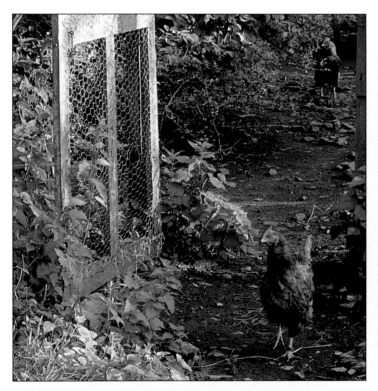

Free-ranging hens *There is something very comforting about having some hens about the place. Allowing them free range is ideal, although they should be limited by netting.*

Cows *A neighboring farmer might agree to using your land as extra grazing. Prize Jersey cows such as these, however, are likely to remain a visual delight on his side of the fence.*

STORAGE BUILDINGS

For the practical country gardener, a storage shed is rather like the kitchen of a traditional home—it is the place where all the important day-to-day functions happen. It deserves to be ordered, to provide a practical, dry place for expensive tools that need maintenance and cleaning after use. Lawn mowers in particular need constant care if they are not to give up.

It is items like canes, stakes and hoses that clutter a storage space very quickly. My particular aversion is the new type of plastic hose that twists and does not roll up neatly! There is also the evergrowing mountain of flower pots we can't bear to throw away. The terracotta pots feel so nice, and will probably become collectors' items soon. Then there are the unfinished sacks of this and that, compost or bonemeal for instance. Ideally they need their own bins. But more important is the safe storage of lethal sprays and weedkillers, which should be stored high and locked up, away from children and/or pets.

LOGS FOR FUEL

The wise countryman buys in—or saves up his wood a year in advance, keeping it neatly stored and drying out for the following winter. If he is really smart he buys in kindling wood, intermediate-size logs and then hefty Yule-tide ones, and stores them separately. He should also have pinned up nearby the following lines to remind him of the qualities of the different woods he can burn.

Beechwood fires are bright and clear, if the logs are kept a year;
Oaken logs burn steadily, if the wood is old and dry.
Chestnut's only good, they say, if for long it's laid away.
But ash new or old
Is fit for a Queen with a crown of gold.

Birch and fir logs burn too fast—blaze up bright, but do not last.
Make a fire of elder tree, death within your house you'll see.
It is by the Irish said hawthorn bakes the sweetest bread.
But ash green or ash brown
Is fit for a Queen with a golden crown.

Elm wood burns like churchyard mould—e'en the very flames
are cold.

Poplar gives a bitter smoke, fills your eyes and makes you choke.
Apple wood will scent your room, with an incense-like perfume.
But ash wet or ash dry
For a Queen to warm her slippers by.   (Author unknown)

Open-sided shelter (right) *Traditional tools are beautiful and this open-sided tool shed makes a real feature of them.*

Tool shed extension (below) *A small open barn built as an extension to a tool shed makes a useful all-purpose storage area.*

THE HERB GARDEN

Herbs, particularly their medicinal properties, have been written about since Roman times, but not until the late twentieth century have they received quite so much attention. Perhaps this is in reaction to their rejection during the nineteenth century and the early part of this one, in favor of newly discovered "scientific" medi-cations. None of the properties of herbs advocated for generations has changed, but since we are now concerned about taking too much synthetic chemical into our bodies, we have turned to the medicinal, culinary, cosmetic and odoriferous qualities of herbs with a new vengeance.

INFORMAL USE OF HERBS
Think of the herb garden, and many are drawn to the idea of formal schemes, including knot gardens, where herbs have to be constantly tended and clipped to maintain intricate patterns. Although these can be successful when linked to a grand and formal building, there is no requirement to use herbs in this way. Such a usage is in the tradition of the enclosed garden that turns its back on nature.

Many gardeners include herbs amongst their plantings quite unconsciously—rosemary for instance, lavender, rue, many of the gray-leaved plants and so on. But the new-look country garden does not include such time-consuming features as herbaceous borders; rather, it uses all its plants, including herbs, in a far less conscious manner. There are plants for scent that you brush against, chamomiles to walk upon, and groupings that will attract insects and butterflies. Then there is the culinary collection of herbs, planted in pleasing combinations both by the kitchen door, and amongst your vegetables.

Shropshire herb garden
(right) *Chives* (Allium schoenoprasum), *one of the smallest of the onion family, are massed together in this garden.*

Herby window-sill
(left) *This herbal harvest includes garlic cloves, rosemary and thyme, and marinating herbal vinegars. The little bundles are home-made* bouquet garni.

THE VERSATILITY OF HERBS

Herbs growing as companion plants to other food crops may well have a beneficial effect while they are growing. One theory suggests that certain herbal scents, root excretions and other plant exhalations will deter insect pests. It is a fact that herbs themselves are seldom attacked by them. Nasturtiums, for instance, are said to deter aphids, while tansy and southernwood ward off fruit moth, and garlic and other alliums protect most garden plants from a variety of pests. Wormwood and rue are even said to discourage animal pests such as slugs and moles. By considering carefully which plants to grow together, you can promote healthy growth, using a completely natural form of pest control.

NATURAL DYES

There is a range of herbs that provide natural dyes of a depth and luster that no synthetic dye can match (woad for blue, for example, madder for red and chamomile for yellow). Wool is the preferred fibre for natural dyes as it achieves an even take; some country gardeners dye the wool from their own paddock sheep. However, other natural fibres, such as cotton and linen, also color well so growing herbs for dying is doubly worthwhile.

Biennial dyer's woad Isatis tinctoria, *foreground, is an ancient blue dye plant, while angelica (*Angelica archangelica, *behind*) *may be used for flavoring fish in several dishes.*

Sweet cicely (Myrrhis odorata) *The stems of sweet cicely can be chopped up and stewed with fruit as a sugar substitute. The seeds of the plant can also be used as a flavoring—they taste of liquorice.*

Thyme (Thymus *sp.*) *The most common of the aromatic herbs, thyme is used particularly with Mediterranean food. Its pungency blends with garlic, olives, tomatoes and the wines of Southern cuisine.*

Parsley (Petroselinum crispum) *There are many forms of parsley—this is the curled-leafed form that is so useful for garnishes and in salads. Its flavor is subtler than that of Italian parsley (see p.183).*

Dill (Anethum graveolens) *Dill is a hardy annual. The leaves are used in much Scandinavian cooking, particularly with fish, while its seeds taste of caraway and are used for seasoning.*

Sage (Salvia officinalis) *Sage tends to be overused with fatty foods, but is excellent with sausage meat and as a flavoring with cheeses (Derby and Vermont). An infusion makes a good gargle for a sore throat.*

Chamomile (Chamaemelum nobile) *Chamomile is useful as a grass substitute for lawns. A non-flowering form, C.n. 'Treneague', is best for lawns as the flat effect is lost when the plants flower.*

HERB PLANTING

Herbs will grow in most soils, as long as they are in full sun. The selection becomes restricted if your soil is extremely acid or alkaline, but if it is generally poor, take heart; herbs prefer this to a rich soil. There is a limited range of herbs for damp and shady positions.

For normal household culinary use your herbs need to be close to hand, combining quite large numbers of some plants, but only a few of others. It depends on your cooking. For myself a little sage goes a very long way, while I use masses of chives, sorrel, basil, tarragon, parsley and mint.

You may plant up these masses in blocks or grow them in a random manner. Intersperse them with the odd rosemary or even a shrub rose and your culinary bed instantly becomes decorative. To extend the decorative content, consider the contrasting colors of herb foliage that you might incorporate. There are the golds of varieties of marjoram, feverfew, thyme and sage, and then the much larger range of silver- and gray-leaved plants, the artemisias, lavenders and mints, and also sage, rue and santolina. The final ingredient should be tones of purple foliage, choosing from bronze fennel, purple sage, black peppermint, and purple basil.

Herb garden in autumn *The herb garden in autumn is past its best, but late summer sun illuminates the foliage colors and textures of purple sage (foreground), with rosemary beyond.*

HERB PLANTING SCHEME

This is a planting scheme for a small herb garden, outside the kitchen door, next to the sunniest corner of a house. The terrace is of stone slab with a brick paver infill, and occasional stone slabs are positioned throughout the garden from which to pick. Big masses of useful culinary herbs are mixed with more decorative shrubby ones, so that the mixture has form and interest through the year. The herbs are allowed to run off into the gravel surround at the outer edges of the garden. Mints are restricted to pots since they are so invasive.

4 Mullein (Verbascum bombyciferum)

3 Purple sage (Salvia officinalis 'Purpurascens')

1 White-flowering shrub rose (Rosa 'Dupontii')

4 Bronze fennel (Foeniculum vulgare)

8 Catmint (Nepeta cataria)

2 Rosemary

French tarragon mass

4 Hyssop (Hyssopus officinalis)

4 Orris (Iris × germanica var. florentina)

2 Golden sage (Salvia officinalis 'Aurea')

Lemon mint (Mentha × piperita citrata)

Hop

Basil mass (Ocimum basilicum)

Parsley mass

1 Angelica (Angelica archangelica)

1 Apple mint (Mentha suaveolens)

Chive mass

3 Curry plants (Helichrysum angustifolium)

Pot marigolds (Calendula officinalis)

4 Lady's mantle (Alchemilla mollis)

1 Globe artichoke (Cynara scolymus)

Sorrel mass (Rumex acetosa)

2 Angelica (Angelica arthangelica)

Climbing rose

10 Silver thyme (Thymus lanuginosus)

1 Alchemilla mollis

1 Rosemary (Rosmarinus offficinalis 'Miss Jessup's Upright')

THE GARDEN IN AUTUMN

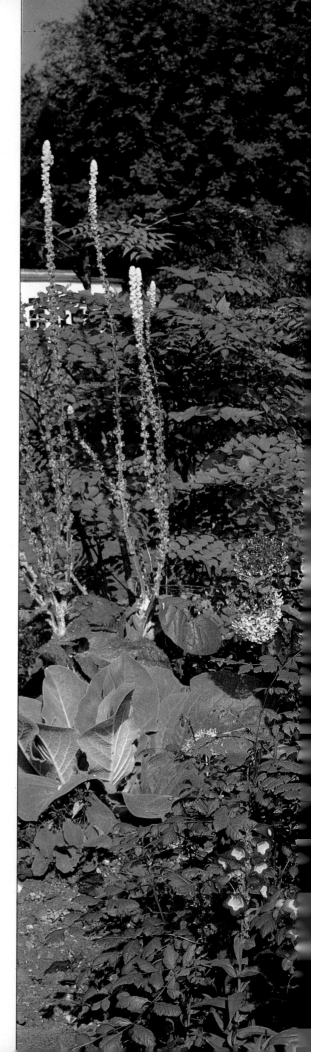

Autumn is a time of action in the country garden. Just as in nature all is gathered and stored for winter use, so in the garden the summer crops are harvested, and flowers hung up to dry. Logs are sawn, jams are made and the garden tidied and virtually "put to bed" for winter. It is a season of satisfaction for the job well done, completed against the honeyed background of harvested fields.

As the plough follows the harvester, the country-gardener follows the harvest by digging, so that frost action can have its beneficial effect on the soil, and compost spreading amongst the shrubs to feed and shelter their roots through the coming winter months.

PLANNING AND PLANTING

Autumn is also the time for planning and planting, not just the spring bulbs but also trees and shrubs. These days, when we buy most new plants container-grown and ready for planting at any time of year, as long as the ground is neither frost bound nor gripped by drought, we tend to forget that autumn is the traditional time for planting shrubs and trees. At one time larger plants were dug for you by the grower (sometimes this is still the case with trees) and at this time of year the exposed and cut roots had the best chance of recovery. For this reason autumn is still the best time for repositioning a youthful shrub, or even moving a tree, especially if you have prepared it a month or so beforehand, using a spade to partially isolate from the surrounding earth the largest amount of earth you can move with the specimen.

Gardening is a transitory craft, and in autumn the anticipation of next year's scene is a spur to improve on the results of the summer past.

Autumn labors (left) *Autumn is the time for cutting back, burning or composting the spent season's growth, and rationalizing what remains.*

The last blooms of summer (right) *Autumn sunlight has a unique glowing quality that here illuminates foreground penstemon against the bold leaves of* Viburnum rhytidophyllum.

HERBS FOR DRYING

Here is a selection of herbs, some freshly picked, others dried, all of which can be grown in the country garden. They are beautiful plants for inclusion in a decorative, mixed planting scheme, but they are also invaluable in the home. Their cultivation could not be easier—most like to be hot and dry.

Bay (Laurus nobilis) *Use dried for flavoring, individually and in bouquet garni*

Tarragon (Artemisia dracunculus)

Basil (Ocimum basilicum 'Minimum') *For salads, sauces and cheeses*

Chives (Allium schoenoprasum) *A classic component of fines herbes*

Rosemary (Rosmarinus officinalis) *Use particularly with lamb*

Sage (Salvia officinalis) *Use in stuffings and cheeses. Infuse purple sage (S.o.'Purpurascens') for a throat gargle*

Thyme (Thymus sp.) *Use the leaves of woody thymes in bouquet garni and for general seasoning*

Dill (Anethum graveolens) *Use this feathery annual with salad and pickle, fish and poultry*

Pot marjoram (Origanum onites) *Leaves used to season meat and vegetables*

German chamomile (Matricaria chamomilla) *Use the dried flowers to make a calming tea*

French sorrel (Rumex scutatus) *For soups, salads and sauces*

Chervil (Anthriscus cerefolium) *Mild licorice flavor and good with egg dishes*

Curled parsley (Petroselineum crispum) *Pretty but less flavor than Italian flat-leaf type*

Bouquet garni *Parsley stalks, sprigs of thyme and marjoram, and a bay leaf, all in a twist of muslin*

Coriander (Coriandrum sativum) *Include in soups and stews*

THE ESSENCE OF AUTUMN

The passing of the autumnal equinox is the prelude to strong sidelight as the sun's daily path sinks towards the horizon. The details of the garden are brought into high relief, shadows are longer and leaves and stems are back-lit. In the evenings, falling temperatures make a fire a welcome thing again. The wider gap between day and night temperatures makes dews heavy, covering every detail in crystal droplets.

The gardener's presence is often denoted by spires of gray smoke rising out of the greenery, for it is time to burn up the summer surpluses of spent growth and the first fallen leaves, where such burning is allowed. Asters gleam in low sunlight, and dahlia blooms ignore the countdown to the first frost. All sad in a way, but it is a time of blackberry picking and swathes of heather upon the moor.

Heavy dews and long shadows *Autumn is a poignant time of dew-dropped cob-webs in the early mornings (right) and long afternoon shadows (below).*

Orchard tidy (opposite) *With summer's growth over, tidying can start, including cutting back and grubbing out if necessary.*

APPLES

The apple tree (*Malus sylvestris*), in its multifarious varieties
that bear fruits pleasing to both the eye and the palate, is hardly
ever out of place in a country garden. Saplings are a joy to nurture,
while gnarled old beauties are to be treasured.

Baker's Delicious *Pick when
orange-red flush appears. Maintains
its flavor for about three weeks
and requires gentle handling*

St Edmund's Russet
*Crisp and juicy, maintaining its
distinctly russet flavor
for about three weeks*

Red Ellison *Keeps crisp for a
fortnight, then mellows, developing
a strong aniseed scent and flavor*

Worcester Pearmain *A properly
ripe Worcester is half bright red,
sweet and crunchy. Best picked
as required*

Queen Cox *A richly
colored and flavored
type of Cox that lasts a full
three months after picking*

Lobo *The deep red skin contrasts
with a white juicy flesh of meringue-
like texture. Ideal for salads,
baking and sauce*

Sunset *Juicy, but a
solid, "meaty" apple with
a rich, tangy flavor
and characteristic sunset-
like coloring*

Ribston Pippin *Reputed to be a
parent of the Cox apple, with a
strong, spicy flavor that develops
with the brick-red flush, and matures
through the winter*

Orleans Reinette A large, spicy russet apple that flushes orange when ripe in late autumn. Rich, nutty flavor with a grainy texture

Cornish Gilliflower Conspicuously ribbed. Pick as maroon flush develops for delicious, crisp, sweet, full-bodied eating

Michaelmas Red Deep red skin and tender, white flesh that is juicy and mildly sweet. Small unless thinned in early summer

Merton Joy A showy, mid-season apple. Crisp and fairly sharp as it ripens, but quickly mellows as it develops a vague spicy flavor

Arthur Turner (Cooking) Pick the largest weekly from high summer to early winter. An excellent baker

Warner's King (Cooking) At its best in early winter. Good for apple dumplings

Monarch (Cooking) Slightly "dented" all over its shiny surface. Excellent for mincemeat and good for grilling

Woolbrook Russet (Cooking) A dull green, acid cooker that is as versatile as a Bramley. Its Russet skin wrinkles through the winter

Bramley (Cooking) This celebrated apple is not invariably green, it sometimes sports a cheerful crimson flush. Susceptible to frost damage

AUTUMN COLOR

The intensity of autumn color alters from year to year according to the weather (a sharp fall in temperature producing a more fleeting but more brilliant foliage display) and from region to region depending on the nature of the location and its soil. On acid soils, for example, reds are particularly deep, while on limy ones, leaves of field maples and mountain ash have a yellower look. In general, autumn color in the north of England is far more subtle with the delicate golds of birches and purple patches upon the moors predominating.

COLORED FRUITS

Much of the richness of autumnal color is provided by fruit—not necessarily the edible kind, although a heavily laden apple orchard with autumn sun upon it is a sight to behold and worth a place in any country garden.

Amongst smaller decorative garden trees, varieties of mountain ash (*Sorbus aucuparia*) provide a whole range of colored berries from the pink/white ones of *S.a.* 'Cashmiriana', through the yellow and amber of *S.a.* 'Joseph Rock', to the scarlet of *S.a.* 'Matsumurana', the Japanese mountain ash. Then there are the delightful fruits of crab apples, the *Malus* genus. *Malus* 'Gold Hornet' fairly glows until mid-winter, while the orange/scarlet, conical fruits of *Malus* 'John Downie' make wonderful jelly. *Malus* 'Red Sentinel' produces massive clusters of cardinal red fruit that last right into spring.

Viburnums, pyracantha and cotoneasters together provide a huge range of berry colors and tones (blues, oranges, reds and yellows), on shrubs or climbing plants that will suit many country locations.

Late autumn sunlight (right) *Here, late autumn sunlight falls on a row of poplars with a hornbeam (*Carpinus *sp.) hedge glowing beyond. Like beech, hornbeam retains its leaves in winter.*

Side light (below left) *It is the strong light from the autumn sun that throws color into strong relief against deep shade. Here, an aged beech gives way to a sun-drenched mass of shrubs.*

Orange-berried pyracantha (below) *The firethorn (*Pyracantha *spp. and cus.), is a close relative of the many varieties of cotoneaster. All are laden with white flowers in early summer and then have the bonus of spectacularly colored berries in autumn.*

HARVEST VEGETABLES

If anything is to inspire the gourmet within us, it is surely an array of vegetable garden produce such as this, beautiful at harvest time, when growing, and in the pot. The kitchen garden is a place where you can fuse decorative with practical gardening.

Jerusalem artichoke (Helianthus tuberosus) *Tasty tubers that make fine soup*

Salsify (Tragopogon porrifolius) *Known as vegetable oyster, owing to the taste of the cooked roots*

Sweet corn (Zea mays) *To be planted in blocks of short rows for both looks and fertilization*

Beet (Beta vulgaris) *A vegetable or salad crop, the globe-rooted form being most useful*

Turnip (Brassica rapa) *A purple-top variety, picked young for its tender flesh*

Field mushroom (Psalliota campestris) *A tasty bonus that accompanies misty autumnal mornings*

Carrot (Daucus carota) *A slender, tapering variety for use raw or cooked*

Onion (Allium cepa) *Two varieties from the several classes of an indispensible vegetable*

Kohl-rabi (Brassica oleracea caulorapa) *Requires moisture during growth*

Purple cauliflower (Brassica oleracea italica) *Easier and hardier than white cauliflower*

Broccoli (Brassica oleracea italica) *Nutritious and flavorful and freezes well*

Round zucchini (Cucurbita pepo) *A vegetable of great culinary versatility*

Celeriac (Apium graveolens rapaceum) *Tasty turnip-rooted celery*

Pumpkin (Cucurbita maxima), (right), and winter squash (C. pepo cv.) *For autumn harvest and can be stored*

Zucchini (Cucurbita pepo) *Best cut when small to medium in size*

AUTUMN TIDY-UP

Long before autumn is officially over, many garden tasks seem very wintery. The general sweep, clean and burn up, for instance, and the spreading and light forking through of compost or well-rotted farmyard manure. It is the best time for sorting and moving many plants, dividing them where necessary. The temptation is to leave the job until spring but by then herbaceous perennials will be unrecognizable, if showing at all.

Only cut back those shrubs that are truly hardy in your region. Last year's straggling growths (of established lavenders for instance) will help to protect plants from heavy frosts through winter.

Dividing perennials (right) *When dividing plants use two forks to pry apart fibrous perennial root masses. If this fails, or if the root is tuberous take a spade and chop it through.*

Autumn bonfires (below) *Bonfire time in the orchard (against the law in most regions today) is all part of the autumn tidy-up. Your overall aim should be to create the neat put-to-bed look of a winter garden.*

GARDEN CASE HISTORIES

The plans shown on the following pages
represent a number of my designs for country gardens. The
purpose of one of them (see p. 195) is to introduce new country
style to a town plot for a relaxed, easy-to-maintain look.
The remainder, in country locations, display a host of
problems that commonly occur and can be solved in many
different ways to suit the requirements of the garden's users.
You may find some inspiration here when it comes
to planning your own layout.

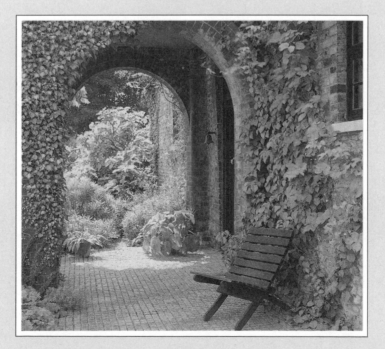

ADDING PRIVACY TO A GARDEN

One problem facing this large garden was a lack of privacy. On the north side of the cottage there is a charming view up a reach of stream with a public right of way on its opposite bank. The south side of the cottage borders a road. The front door was rarely used since the only access to it was via a small path leading from the road. The kitchen door on the east side was used instead. The new garden has been redirected away from the stream towards a beautiful meadow full of flowers. A new yew hedge screens the garden from the road and forecourt, while the public right of way beyond the stream to the north is hidden by

Existing fence

Oak tree

Mixed shrub planting screens the garden from the stream

Stream

Deck

Front door

Gravel drive opens up the area at the south of the cottage

Hazel tree

Existing forsythia

Decorative shrub planting

Meadow containing wild flowers and grasses

Mown lawn

Yew hedge makes an effective screen

Herb border

Flower borders

Gravel forecourt

Cottage

Store

Entrance to cottage

Mixed shrubs and perennials

Climbing shrubs screen the cottage from the road

Sheltered paved terrace

TOWN GARDEN

shrub planting. A gravel drive has been added along the south side of the house to allow access to the front door, and a vegetable garden is now located away from the house, screened by a box hedge.

The requirements for this small town garden are that it should involve little maintenance and look spacious. It has been redesigned to incorporate a new but "distressed" natural look. The lawn has been replaced with a stone-paved terrace and different levels of gravel containing random planting. Large stepping stones link the areas. A partially concealed grassy play area has been created at the bottom of the garden.

Box hedge screens
Vegetable garden

Vegetable garden located
away from the cottage

Barn

Cobbled surface

Oak tree

Grassy play area
for children

Random shrub
planting

Garden seat
in the shade of
the pear tree

Hedge screens
rough grass

Tubs of lilies

Large pear tree

Bay tree

Raised gravel
area with
random
planting

Decorative shrub
planting

Garden wall

Conifer screens
neighboring
wall

Brick step up

Stepping stones
link terrace to
gravel area

Open loggia
stores garden
furniture

Perennial flower bed

Old York stone terrace
with brick infill

PRACTICAL AND NATURAL STYLE

The owners of this garden wanted a practical garden style involving little fuss and maintenance. So a soft and slightly wild approach was adopted, which works well in such a garden of less than 2.5 hectares (an acre).

A brick terrace has been built near the house, which is brightened with tubs of flowers. This leads on to a mown lawn and beyond this the view is directed towards some existing old fruit trees and bold swathes of rough grass planted with spring bulbs. A grassy mound edged with evergreens adds further interest. At the side of the house is a play area, with low-maintenance shrub planting at the front for year-round decoration.

Rough grass containing spring bulbs

Existing fruit trees

Circular bench seat around fruit tree

Evergreen planting

Weeping willow

Low brick wall screens storage area

Contoured grassy berm

Paved area for storage

Brick paved terrace

Pond

Garage

Herb garden

Sunroom

Grassy play area

House

Pyracantha hedge

Gravel

Low-maintenance shrub planting

UTILIZING THE AVAILABLE SPACE

This house has a large area of land but only a small portion of it was used as a garden. This was behind the house, raised about 1.5m (4 ft) above ground level. It was a walled garden surrounded by tall neighboring trees, which made it claustrophobic. The land to the south of the house was used as a random car parking area, restricting the view of a delightful barn.

The garden has now been extended. A terrace overlooks a new lawn and commands a view of the barn. A new rear entrance has been built and cars are restricted to this end of the yard. The walled garden is now a place for shrub roses and species bulbs growing in long grass.

Paved sitting area

Steps up to walled garden area

Shrub roses

Mown grass

Garden seat

Flowering cherry tree

Rough grass planted with wildflowering bulbs

House

Gravel

York stone paving

New paved terrace with south-facing view

Flowering cherry tree

Screen planting

Entrance

Pine trees

Gravel parking area

New mown lawn

Gravel drive

Specimen acer

Existing shrub planting

OPENING UP A VIEW

This manor house has a large garden that was very formal and structured. The aim was to soften the design of the garden to make it more in tune with the surrounding countryside. The approach to the manor house has been left formal: a gravelled forecourt planted with plane trees. At the rear, a new L-shaped ha-ha allows an unrestricted view from the house out on to parkland. Elements of rougher grass have been introduced to frame the house and to help screen a swimming pool area at the side of the garden. The detailing round the house is now bolder and simpler, with wide stone terraces and rich shrub planting.

Rough grass containing a clump of trees

L-shaped ha-ha allows an open view of parkland

Swimming pool screened from house

Rough grass containing bulbs and a clump of trees

Grassy bank slopes gently down to mown lawn

York stone terrace containing random planting

Oak tubs containing clipped trees

Manor house

Small formal garden with flower borders

Climbers soften the exterior of the house

Formal gravel forecourt

Gravel path

London plane trees

RE-ORIENTATING A GARDEN

This house has a fine view south over cultivated fields. However, between the house and the fields was a fence and an ugly gravel car-turn, so the view could not be easily appreciated. It was decided to re-orientate the garden. So a more practical gravel forecourt has been created at the rear of the house and the original car-turn made into a lawn. Removing the boundary fence to the field now allows an open view from the house, which can be enjoyed from a new brick terrace built to overlook the fields. A copse of silver birch trees replaces the original gravel drive. The edges of the lawn are softened with rough grass containing bulbs.

Rough grass planted with spring-flowering bulbs

Existing paving

Entrance to house

House

Carport

New gravel forecourt

Lavender border

Bench seat around thorn tree

Field under cultivation

Field boundary

Original car-turn made into a lawn

Brick terrace overlooking fields

Copse planting of silver birch trees in rough grass

Existing pine trees

View down avenue

PLANTS FOR A NATURAL LOOK

*The following lists are a guide
to finding plants that match your country location rather
than clash with it. If you choose carefully, you will
achieve a special harmony between the plants within your
boundaries and those beyond. The plants are a mixture of
native species, species that have become naturalized despite
originating abroad, and plants, that although exotic,
have a sufficiently "wild" look to suit a country style.
Included are plants for mild climates as well
as colder regions.*

Walnut—a native tree

TREES

Acer campestre Field maple
Acer griseum Paperbark maple
Acer negundo Box elder
Acer pensylvanicum Moosewood
Aesculus hippocastanum Horse chestnut
Aesculus parviflora Buckeye
Alnus cordata Italian alder
Alnus glutinosa Black alder
Alnus incana Gray alder
Amelanchier spp. Shadbush
Betula lenta Sweet birch
Betula pendula Silver birch
Betula pubescens Downy birch
Carpinus betulus European hornbeam
Cornus florida Flowering dogwood
Cornus kousa chinensis Chinese
   dogwood
Corylus avellana Hazel
Crataegus spp. and cvs. Hawthorn
Fagus grandifolia American beech
Fraxinus excelsior European ash
Ilex aquifolium English holly
Ilex opaca American holly
Juglans cinerea Butternut
Malus spp. Crab apple
Nyssa sylvatica Tupelo
Oxydendrum arboreum Sourwood
Parrotia persica
Pinus strobus White pine

Pinus sylvestris Scots pine
Populus canescens Gray poplar
Populus tremula Aspen
Prunus avium Sweet cherry
Prunus padus Bird cherry
Prunus virginiana Chokeberry
Pyrus communis Pear
Quercus alba White oak
Quercus coccinea Scarlet oak
Quercus palustris Pin oak
Quercus robur English oak
Quercus rubra Red oak
Quercus virginiana Southern live oak
Robinia pseudoacacia Black locust
Rhus typhina Staghorn sumach
Salix alba White willow
Salix caprea Goat willow
Salix cinerea Gray willow
Salix pentandra Bay willow
Salix viminalis Osier
Sassafras albidum Sassafras
Sorbus aria Whitebeam
Sorbus aucuparia Mountain ash
Styrax japonica Japanese styrax
Taxus baccata Yew
Tilia americana American linden
Tilia cordata European linden
Tilia platyphyllos Large-leaved linden
Tsuga canadensis Canada hemlock
Viburnum lantana Wayfaring tree
Viburnum lentago Sheepberry

Honeysuckle—a climbing shrub

SHRUBS

Acer campestre Field maple
Aronia arbutifolia Red chokeberry
Buxus sempervirens Box
Calluna vulgaris and cvs. Heather, ling
Clethra alnifolia Summer sweet
Cornus alba Tartarian
Cornus mas Cornelian cherry
Cornus sanguinea Blood-twig dogwood
Corylopsis spicata Winter hazel
Corylus avellana Hazel
Crataegus spp. Hawthorn
Cytisus scoparius Broom
Daphne laureola Spurge laurel
Erica spp. and cvs. Heath
Euonymus alata Winged euonymus
Hamamelis spp. and cvs. Witch hazel
Hippophae rhamnoides Sea buckthorn
Hydrangea quercifolia Oaklcaf hydrangea
Ilex glabra Inkberry
Juniperus virginiana Red-cedar
Kalmia latifolia Mountain-laurel
Lindera benzoin Spicebush
Myrica pensylvanica Bayberry
Pieris floribunda Fetterbush
Rhododendron spp. and cvs. Rhododendron and azalea
Rhamnus cathartica Common buckthorn
Rhamnus frangula Alder buckthorn
Rhus copallina Shining sumach
Rosa arvensis Field rose
Rosa canina Dog rose
Rosa eglanteria Sweetbrier
Rosa multiflora Fence rose
Ruscus aculeatus Butcher's broom
Salix cinerea Gray willow
Salix purpurea Purple willow
Salix viminalis Osier
Sambucus canadensis American elderberry
Symphoricarpus albus Snowberry
Vaccinium spp. Blueberry, bilberry, cranberry
Viburnum acerifolium Maple-leaf viburnum
Viburnum opulus Guelder rose
Viburnum setigerum Tea viburnum
Viburnum wrightii Wright's viburnum

Rosa rugosa
'Frau Dagmar Hastrup'

SHRUB ROSES

Rosa hugonis Father Hugo rose
Rosa nitida Shining rose
Rosa roxburghii Roxburgh rose
Rosa rubrifolia Redleaf rose
Rosa rugosa 'Alba'
Rosa rugosa 'Frau Dagmar Hastrup'
Rosa rugosa 'Max Graf'
Rosa rugosa 'Sir Thomas Lipton'
Rosa wichuraiana Memorial rose

BAMBOOS AND GRASSES

BAMBOOS

Arundinaria simonii
Arundinaria variegata
Arundinaria viridistriata
Phyllostachys aureasulcata Yellowgroove bamboo
Phyllostachys flexuosa
Phyllostachys nigra Black bamboo
Phyllostachys nigra 'Henon' Henon bamboo
Phyllostachys viridi-glaucescens

GRASSES

Agrostis stolonifera Creeping bent
Agrostis tenuis Colonial bent
Alopecurus pratensis Meadow foxtail

Quaking grass—
a naturalized grass

Arundo donax Giant reed
Avena fatua Oat grass
Bouteloua gracilis Mesquite grass
Briza media Quaking grass
Calamagrostis × *acutiflorus* 'Stricta'
  Feather reed grass
Calamagrostis × *acuitifloras*
  'Karl Foerster'
Carex conica Sedge
Carex morrowii 'alba' Blue grass
Carex morrowii 'Variegata' Blue
  grass
Cortaderia selloana Pampas grass
Cortaderia selloana 'Rosea' Pink
  pampas grass
Deschampsia caespitosa Tufted hair
  grass
Deschampsia flexuosa Hair grass
Elymus arenarius Lyme grass
Festuca amethystina Fescue grass
Festuca elatior Reed fescue
Festuca ovina 'Glauca' Blue fescue
Festuca rubra Red fescue
Festuca tenuifolia Hair fescue
Helictotrichon sempervirens Blue oat
  grass
Holcus lanatus Velvet grass
Hordeum vulgare Common barley
Koeleria spp. Hair grass
Lolium perenne Perennial ryegrass
Milium effusum Wood millet

Miscanthus sinensis 'Gracillimus'
  Eulalia
Miscanthus sinensis 'Purpurascencs'
Miscanthus sinensis 'Variegatus'
Miscanthus sinensis 'Zebrinus' Zebra
  grass
Molinia caerulea 'Variegata' Purple
  moor grass
Pennisetum alopecuroides Chinese
  fountain grass
Pennisetum setaceum Fountain grass
Phalaris arundinacea 'Picta'
  Gardener's garters
Phleum pratense Timothy
Poa pratensis Kentucky bluegrass
Poa trivialia Rough meadow grass
Spartina pectinata Prairie cordgrass
Stipa gigantea Feather grass
Uniola latifolia

GROUNDCOVER PLANTS

DRY SHADED AREAS
Acanthus balcanicus Bear's breeches
Acanthus mollis Artist's acanthus
Aegopodium podagraria Goutweed
Alchemilla vulgaris Lady's mantle
Anaphalis triplinervis Life-everlasting
Berberis verruculosa Barberry
Brunnera macrophylla Siberian bugloss
Convalleria majalis Lily-of-the-valley
Epimedium spp. and cvs. Barrenwort
Euonymus fortunei and cvs.
  winter-creeper
Gaylussacia spp. Huckleberry
Hedera spp. and cvs. Ivy
Hypericum calycinum St John's-wort
Lamium spp. and cvs. Dead-nettle
Liriope spp. and cvs. Lily-turf
Lonicera japonica and cvs. Japanese
  honeysuckle
Mahonia repens Oregon grape
Nepeta hederacea Ground-ivy
Omphalodes cappadocica
Pachysandra terminalis
Parthenocissus quinquefolia Virginia
  creeper
Paxistima (Pachystima) canbyi Cliff
  green
Polygonatum spp. Solomon's seal

Polygonum spp. Knotweed
Polystichum acrostichoides Christmas
  fern
Pulmonaria spp. and cvs. Lungwort
Sarcococca hookeriana Sweet box
Stachys spp. Woundwort
Symphoricarpos spp. Snowberry
Vaccinium angustifolium Low-bush
  blueberry
Vinca minor Periwinkle
Waldsteinia spp.

MOIST SHADED AREAS
Ajuga spp.and cvs. Bugleweed
Alchemilla vulgaris Lady's-mantle
Asarum spp. Wild ginger
Astrantia spp. Masterwort
Bergenia spp.
Convalleria majalis Lily-of-the-valley
Cornus canadensis Bunchberry
Dryopteris spp. Woodfern
Epimedium spp. Barrenwort
Galax ureolata Wandflower
Gaultheria spp. and cvs
Gaylussacia brachycera Box
  huckleberry
Hosta spp. and cvs. Plantain lily
Houttuynia cordata 'Variegata'
Leucothoe fontanesiana
Lysimachia spp. Loosestrife
Mitchella repens Partridge-berry
Polygonatum spp. Solomon's seal

Field forget-me-not—
a hedgerow annual

Polygonum spp. Knotgrass
Primula spp. and cvs. Primrose
Pulmonaria spp. Lungwort
Salix spp. Willow
Sarcococca hookeriana Sweet box
Tiarella cordifolia Foamflower
Vinca minor Periwinkle

WILDLIFE FOOD PLANTS

TREES AND SHRUBS
Amelanchier spp. Shadblow
Arbutus spp. Strawberry tree
Arctostaphylos uva-ursi Bearberry
Aronia arbutifolia Red chokeberry
Aucuba japonica Spotted laurel
Benzoin aestivale Spicebush
Berberis spp. Barberry
Buddleia spp. Butterfly bush
Callicarpa 'Profusion'
Carissa grandiflora Natal-plum
Celastrus scandens Bittersweet
Chaenomeles spp. Flowering quince
Chionanthus virginicus Fringetree
Clerodendrum trichotomum
Colutea arborescens Bladder senna
Cornus spp. and cvs. Dogwood
Corylus avellana Common hazel
Corylus maxima 'Purpurea' Filbert
Cotoneaster spp. and cvs.
Crataegus spp. and cvs. Hawthorn
Daphne mezereum February daphne
Decaisnea fargesii
Dorycnium spp.
Elaeagnus spp. Russian-olive
Euonymus spp. Spindle tree
Feijoa sellowiana Strawberry-guava
Garrya spp. Silk-tassel bush
Gaylussacia brachycera Box
   huckleberry
Gaultheria procumbens Wintergreen
Gaultheria shallon Salal
Hebe spp.
Hippophae rhamnoides Sea buckthorn
Hypericum androsaemum Tutsan
Hypericum forestii St John's-wort
Hypericum indorum 'Elstead'
   St John's-wort
Ilex spp. Holly
Juniperus spp.

Dog violet—
groundcover perennial

Lonicera spp. Honeysuckle
Mahonia spp. and cvs. Oregon grape
Malus spp. Apple and crab apple
Nandina domestica Sacred bamboo
Osmanthus decora
Pernettya mucronata Chilean
   pernettya
Pinus spp. Pine
Photinia spp.
Poncirus trifoliata Hardy orange
Populus nigra Black poplar
Prunus spp. Cherry
Pyracantha spp. Firethorn
Quercus spp. Oak
Rhamnus frangula Alder buckthorn
Rhus typhina Staghorn sumach
Ribes spp. and cvs. Currant and
   gooseberry
Rosa spp. and cvs. Rose
Rubus spp. and cvs. Bramble
Ruscus aculeatus Butcher's broom
Salix spp. Willow
Sambucus spp. Elderberry
Skimmia spp.
Sorbus spp. Rowan
Staphylea spp. Bladdernut
Stranvaesia spp.
Symphoricarpos spp. Snowberry
Syringa spp. Lilac
Taxus spp. Yew
Vaccinium spp. Blueberry, cranberry,
   deerberry, huckleberry
Viburnum spp.
Vitis spp. Grape

GARDEN FLOWERS
Antirrhinum spp. and cvs. Snapdragon
Aster spp. and cvs. Michaelmas daisy
Cosmos spp. and cvs.
Echinops spp. Globe thistle
Helianthus spp. Sunflower
Scabiosa spp. and cvs. Scabious

WILD (WEEDLIKE) PLANTS
Carlina spp. Thistle
Cirsium spp. Thistle
Centaurea nigra Common knapweed
Dipsacus fullonum Teasel
Papaver rhoeas Corn poppy
Senecio jacobaea Ragwort
Tarazacum officinale Dandelion
Urtica dioica Nettle
Vaccinium vitis-idaea Cowberry

PLANTS TO ATTRACT BUTTERFLIES

Achillea millefolium Yarrow
Alliaria petiolata Garlic mustard
Alyssum (Aurinia) spp. and cvs.
   Madwort
Anthyllis vulneraria Kidney vetch
Armeria maritima Thrift
Asclepias tuberosa Butterfly
Aster spp. and cvs. Michaelmas daisy
Aubrieta spp. Purple rock cress
Buddleia spp. and cvs. Butterfly bush
Cardamine pratensis Cuckooflower
Centaurea cyanus Cornflower
Cirsium vulgare Spear thistle
Crataegus monogyna English hawthorn
Cynosurus cristatus Crested dog's-tail
Cytisus scoparius Broom
Dactylis glomerata Cock's-foot
Daucus carota Queen Anne's lace
Dianthus spp. Pink
Erigeron spp. and cvs. Fleabane
Erodium cicutarium Common
   stork's-bill
Eupatorium cannabinum Hemp-
   agrimony
Fragaria vesca Wild strawberry
Gaillardia × grandiflora Blanket
   flower

Poppy—
an insect food plant

Hedera spp. and cvs. Ivy
Helenium autumnale and cvs.
  Sneezeweed
Helianthemum nummularium Common
  rock-rose
Heliotropium aborescens Heliotrope
Hesperis matronalis Dame's-violet
Hippocrepis comosa Horseshoe vetch
Humulus lupulus Wild hop
Hyssopus officinalis Hyssop
Iberis umbellata Annual candytuft
Ilex spp. and cvs. Holly
Lavandula angustifolia Lavender
Ligustrum vulgare Privet
Lindera benzoin Spice bush
Lippia citriodora Lemon verbena
Lobularia maritima and cvs. Sweet-
  alyssum
Lonicera periclymenum Honeysuckle
Lotus corniculatus Common
  bird's-foot-trefoil
Lunaria annua Honesty
Lychnis flos-cuculi Ragged-robin
Lythrum salicaria Purple-loosestrife
Meliotis albus White clover
Myosotis arvensis Field forget-me-not
Nepeta cataria Catmint
Ononis repens Common restharrow
Origanum spp. Marjoram
Petunia cvs.
Phlox paniculata Summer phlox
Plantago lanceolata Ribwort plantain

Poa trivialis Rough meadow-grass
Primula spp. and cvs. Primrose
Prunus spinosa Blackthorn
Quercus robur Oak
Reseda odorata Mignonette
Rhamnus frangula Buckthorn
Rosmarinus officinalis Rosmary
Rubus fruticosus Bramble
Rumex acetosa Common sorrel
Salix caprea Goat willow, pussy willow
Scabiosa spp. and cvs. Scabious
Sedum spectabile Ice plant
Solidago spp. and cvs. Goldenrod
Succisa pratensis Devil's-bit scabious
Syringa spp. and cvs. Lilac
Thymus spp. Thyme
Trifolium repens White clover
Tussilago farfara Colt's foot
Ulex europaeus Gorse
Ulmus procera English elm
Urtica dioica Common nettle
Valeriana officinalis Valerian,
  garden-heliotrops
Veronica chamaedrys Germander
  speedwell
Viola hirta Hairy violet
Viola odorata Sweet violet
Viola riviniana Common dog-violet

White clover—
butterfly food plant

FOOD PLANTS FOR BEES

TREES
Acer spp. and cvs. Maple
Aesculus spp. and cvs. Horse chestnut
Ailanthus altissima Tree-of-heaven
Albizia julibrissin Silk tree
Alnus glutinosa Alder
Alnus incana and cvs. White alder
betula spp. and cvs. Birch
Caragana arborescens Siberian pea tree
Castanea sativa Spanish chestnut
Catalpa bignonioides Indian bean tree
Cotoneaster frigidus
Crataegus spp. and cvs. Hawthorne
Fagus spp. and cvs. Beech
Fraxinus excelsior Common ash
Koelreuteria spp. and cvs. Golden-rain
  tree
Liquidambar styraciflua Sweet gum
Liriodendron tulipifera Tulip tree
Malus spp. and cvs. Apple and crab
  apple
Mespilus germanica Medlar
Nothofagus antarctica Antarctic-beech
Populus nigra Black poplar
Populus tremula Aspen
Prunus spp. and cvs. Plum, cherry
Quercus spp. and cvs. Oak
Robinia pseudoacacia False acacia
Salix spp. Willow
Tilia spp. Lime tree, linden

SHRUBS
Aesculus parviflora Dwarf buckeye
Amelanchier spp. Shadblow
Arbutus spp.
Berberis spp. and cvs. Barberry
Buddleia globosa Butterfly bush
Buxus spp. and cvs. Box
Ceanothus spp.
Cercis siliquastrum Judas tree
Chaenomeles japonica Japanese quince
Colutea spp. Bladder senna
Cornus sanguinea Blood-twig dogwood
Cotoneaster spp. and cvs.
Cytisus spp. and cvs. Broom
Daphne mezereum February daphne
Elaeagnus spp. and cvs.
Escallonia spp. and cvs.
Fuchsia spp. and cvs.

Apple blossom—
food for bees

Helianthemum nummularium Common
  rockrose
Hypericum androsaemum Tutsan
Hypericum forrestii St John's-wort
Ilex spp. and cvs. Holly
Laurus nobilis Sweet bay
Olearia spp. Daisy bush
Prunus laurocerasus and cvs.
  Cherry-laurel
Pyracantha spp. and cvs. Firethorn
Rhamnus frangula Buckthorn
Rhus spp. Sumach
Ribes sanguineum Flowering currant
Ribes speciosum Fuchsia-flowered
  gooseberry
Salix caprea Goat willow
Salix repens argentea Creeping willow
Skimmia japonica Japanese skimmia
Spiraea spp. and cvs.
Staphylea spp. Bladder nut
Stephanandra incisa Lace shrub
Stranvaesia davidiana
Symphoricarpus spp. and cvs.
  Showberry
Syringa spp. and cvs. Lilac
Tamarix 'Pink Cascade' Tamarisk
Ulex europaeus Gorse
Viburnum spp. and cvs.
Weigela spp. and cvs.

PERENNIALS AND ANNUALS

Aconitum napellus Monk's-hood
Allium schoenoprasum Chives
Alyssum (Aurinia) spp. Madwort,
  basket of gold.
Anchusa officinalis Alkanet
Armeria maritima Thrift
Aster spp. and cvs. Michaelmas daisy
Cardamine pratensis Cuckoo flower
Centaurea cyanus Cornflower
Centaurea nigra Common knapweed
Centaurea scabiosa Greater knapweed
Cheiranthus spp. and cvs. Wallflower
Cichorium intybus Chicory
Colchicum spp. Autumn crocus
Coreopsis spp. and cvs. Calliopsis,
  tickseed
Delphinium spp. and cvs. Larkspur
Digitalis purpurea Foxglove
Dipsacus fullonum Teasel
Echinops spp. and cvs. Globe thistle
Echium spp. amd cvs. Viper's bugloss
Endymion spp. English Bluebell,
  wood-hyacinth
Epilobium angustifolium Rosebay
  willowherb
Eryngium maritimum Sea-holly
Eupatorium cannabinum Hemp-
  agrimony
Geranium pratense Meadow crane's-bill
Iberis umbellata Candytuft
Inula spp. Ploughman's-spikenard

Flowering currant—
food for bees

Knautia arvensis Blue buttons
Lamiastrum galeobdolon Yellow
  archangel
Limonium spp. Sea lavender
Lobelia spp. and cvs.
Lobularia maritima Annual alyssum
Lotus corniculatus Common
  bird's-foot-trefoil
Lupinus spp. Lupin
Lythrum salicaria Purple-loosestrife
Malva moschata Musk mallow
Malva sylvestris Common mallow
Melissa officinalis Lemon balm
Mertensia virginica Virginia cowslip
Monarda didyma and cvs. Bee balm
Narcissus spp. and cvs. Daffodil,
  jonquil
Nepeta spp. and cvs. Catmint
Potentilla spp. and cvs. Cinquefoil
Pulmonaria officinalis Lungwort
Ranunculus acris Meadow buttercup
Ranunculus ficaria Lesser celandine
Reseda odorata Mignonette
Salvia officinalis Common sage
Salvia pratensis Meadow clary
Scabiosa spp. and cvs. Pincushion
  flower
Sedum spectabile Ice plant
Senecio spp. Groundsel
Solidago spp. Goldenrod
Succisa pratensis Devil's-bit
Thymus spp. and cvs. Thyme
Tropaeolum spp. Nasturtium
Tussilago farfara Colt's-foot
Verbascum spp. and cvs. Mullein
Veronica spp. and cvs. Speedwell
Viola odorata Sweet violet

RABBIT-RESISTANT PLANTS

TREES AND SHRUBS

Alnus spp. Alder
Arbutus spp.
Aucuba spp. Laurel
Berberis spp. and cvs. Barberry
Betula spp. Birch
Buddleia spp. Butterfly bush
Buxus spp. Box
Ceanothus spp. and cvs.
Choisya ternata Mexican orange
  blossom

Clematis spp. and cvs. Virgin's bower
Cornus sanguinea Dogwood
Cortaderia spp. Pampas grass
Cotoneaster spp. and cvs. (not C. simonsii)

Knotweed—
Unattractive to rabbits

Daphne mezereum February daphne
Deutzia scabra
Elaeagnus pungens 'Maculata'
Fatsia japonica Japanese aralia
Fuchsia spp. and cvs.
Gaultheria spp.
Hippophae rhamnoides Sea buckthorn
Hydrangea spp. and cvs.
Hypericum calycinum Creeping St John's-wort
Ilex spp. and cvs. Holly
Kalmia latifolia Mountain-laurel
Kalmia angustifolia Lambkill, sheep-laurel
Laburnum spp. Goldenchain tree
Ligustrum spp. and cvs. Privet
Lonicera spp. and cvs. Honeysuckle
Olearia spp. Daisy bush
Paeonia spp. and cvs. (tree) Tree paeony
Pernettya mucronata Prickly heath
Philadelphus spp. and cvs. Mock orange
Pinus nigra Austrian pine
Rhododendron spp. and cvs. Rhododendron (low azaleas not immune)
Rhus spp. Sumach

Ribes spp. Currant
Rosa spp. and cvs. (spiny species types) Rose
Rosmarinus spp. Rosemary
Ruscus aculeatus Butcher's broom
Sambucus spp. Elderberry
Skimmia japonica Japanese skimmia
Spiraea spp. and cvs.
Symphoricarpus albus Snowberry
Syringa spp. and cvs. Lilac
Taxus spp. and cvs. Yew
Ulex spp. Gorse
Viburnum lantana Wayfaring tree
Viburnum opulus Guelder rose
Viburnum tinus Laurustinus
Vinca spp. Periwinkle
Yucca spp. Spanish bayonet

PERENNIALS

Acanthus spp. Bear's breeches
Aconitum spp. and cvs. Monkshood
Anemone spp. and cvs. Windflower
Aquilegia spp. and cvs. Columbine
Astilbe spp. and cvs. False goatsbeard
Bergenia spp.
Epimedium spp. and cvs. Barrenwort
Eryngium spp. Eryngo, sea-holly
Euphorbia spp. Spurge
Geranium spp. and cvs. Crane's-bill

Hard fern—
for naturalizing

Helleborus spp. Hellebore
Hemerocallis spp. and cvs. Day-lily
Kniphofia spp. Torch-lily
Lupinus spp. Lupin

Narcissus spp. and cvs. Daffodil, jonquil
Polygonatum spp. Solomon's seal
Polygonum spp. Knotweed
Salvia × *superba* Sage
Saxifraga umbrosa Saxifrage
Sedum spectabile Ice plant

Autumn crocus—
for naturalizing

BULBS FOR NATURALIZING

Allium spp.
Anemone apennina Windflower
Anemone blanda Windflower
Anemone nemorosa Windflower
Brodiaea spp.
Chionodoxa spp. Glory of the snow
Camassia scilloides Wild hyacinth
Colchicum autumnali Autumn crocus
Colchicum speciosum Autumn crocus
Crocus spp. and cvs.
Eranthis hyemalis Winter aconite
Erythronium spp. Dog's tooth-violet
Fritillaria imperialis Crown imperial
Fritillaria meleagris Snake's head fritillary
Fritillaria persica
Galanthus spp. Snowdrop
Leucojum spp. Snowflake
Narcissus spp. and cvs. Daffodil, jonquil
Muscari spp. and cvs. Grape hyacinth
Puschkinia scilloides
Scilla spp. and cvs.
Zephyranthes Rain-lily, zephry-lily

PLANTS FOR COUNTRY MOODS AND PLEASURES

The following plant lists reflect some of the seasonal pleasures of the country garden, encompassing colors, shapes and textures. You will find that most of the plants included will fit into mixed planting schemes admirably, depending on your taste, but if you want to grow large quantities of specific plants to fulfil the requirements of a hobby or other employment, consider growing them separately in bold masses.

COTTAGE GARDEN

Foxglove—
for cottage style

Achillea spp. and cvs. Yarrow
Alcea rosea Hollyhock
Alyssum (Aurinia) spp. Madwort
Amelanchier spp. Shadblow
Anchusa spp. and cvs. Alkanet
Anthyllis vulneraria Kidney vetch
Antirrhinum spp. and cvs. Snapdragon
Aster spp. and cvs. Michaelmas daisy
Aubrieta spp. Purple rock cress
Berberis spp. and cvs. Barberry
Buddleia spp. and cvs. Butterfly bush
Calendula officinalis Pot marigold
Campanula spp. and cvs. Bellflower
Cardamine pratensis Cuckooflower
Centaurea cyanus Cornflower
Centaurea nigra Common knapweed
Chaenomeles speciosa Japanese quince
Cheiranthus spp. and cvs. Wallflower
Cirsium vulgare Spear thistle
Cistus spp. and cvs. Rock-rose
Colchicum spp. and cvs. Autumn-crocus
Colutea arborescens Bladder senna
Consolida ambigua Annual larkspur
Cornus spp. and cvs. Dogwood
Cosmos spp. and cvs.
Cotoneaster spp. and cvs.
Cynosurus cristatus Crested dog's-tail
Dactylis glomerata Cock's-foot

Delphinium spp. and cvs. Larkspur
Dianthus spp. and cvs. Pink, Sweet William
Digitalis purpurea Foxglove
Dipsacus fullonum Teasel
Echinops ritro Globe thistle
Endymion non-scriptus English bluebell, wood-hyacinth
Erodium cicutarium Common stork's-bill
Fragaria vesca Wild strawberry
Godetia (Clarkia) amoena Satin flower
Hedera spp. and cvs. Ivy
Helianthemum nummularium Common rock-rose
Helianthus annuas Sunflower
Hesperis matronalis Sweet rocket
Hippocrepis comosa Horseshoe vetch
Humulus lupulus Wild hop
Hyssopus officinalis Hyssop
Iberis spp. and cvs. Candytuft
Jasminum spp. and cvs. Jasmine
Lathyrus latifolius Everlasting pea
Lathyrus odoratus Sweet pea
Lavandula spp. Lavender
Lippia citriodora Lemon verbena
Lobelia spp. and cvs.
Lonicera periclymenum Honeysuckle
Lotus corniculatus Common bird's-foot-trefoil
Lunaria annua Honesty
Lupinus spp. Lupin
Lychnis flos-cuculi Ragged robin
Lythrum salicaria Purple loosestrife
Malva sylvestris Common mallow
Matthiola bicornis Night-scented stock
Medicago sativa Lucerne, alfalfa
Melissa officinalis Balm
Myosotis arvensis Field forget-me-not
Myosotis sylvatica Garden forget-me-not
Narcissus spp. and cvs. Daffodil, jonquil
Nepeta cataria Catmint
Nepeta × faassenii Garden catmint
Nicotiana spp. and cvs. Tobacco plant
Oenothera biennis Evening primrose
Ononis spp. Common restharrow
Origanum vulgare Marjoram
Petunia cvs.
Phlox paniculata Summer phlox
Plantago lanceolata Ribwort plantain
Primula spp. and cvs. Primrose

Pulmonaria officinalis Lungwort
Ranunculus ficaria Lesser celandine
Reseda odorata Mignonette

Christmas rose—
white-flowering perennial

Rosa spp. and cvs. (scented shrub roses) Rose
Rumex acetosa Common sorrel
Salvia spp. and cvs. Sage
Saponaria officinalis Soapwort
Scabiosa spp. and cvs. Scabious
Sedum spectabile Ice plant
Solidago spp. and cvs. Goldenrod
Thymus spp. and cvs. Thyme
Trifolium repens White clover
Tropaeolum spp. and cvs. Nasturtium
Tussilago farfara Colt's-foot
Valeriana officinalis Common valerian
Verbascum spp. and cvs. Mullein
Veronica spp. and cvs. Speedwell
Viburnum opulus Guelder rose
Viola odorata Sweet violet
Viola tricolor Johnny-jump-up
Viola riviniana Common dog-violet

COLORFUL PERENNIALS

YELLOW/ORANGE

Achillea 'Moonshine' Yarrow
Anthemis tinctoria 'Moonlight' Golden marguerite
Coreopsis verticillata Threadleaf coreopsis

Digitalis grandiflora
Doronicum spp. Leopard's-bane
Euphorbia wulfenii Spurge
Helenium autumnale 'Butterpat'
Heliopsis scabra and cvs. False sunflower
Hemerocallis spp. and cvs. Day-lily
Ligularia dentata 'Desdemona'
Lysimachia punctata Loosestrife
Narcissus spp. and cvs. Daffodil, jonquil
Paeonia mlokosewitschii Peony
Rudbeckia fulgida 'Goldsturm' Coneflower
Verbascum olympicum

BLUE/PURPLE

Aconitum spp. and cvs. Monkshood
Agapanthus Headbourne hybrid African lily
Amsonia tabernaemontana Blue stars
Anchusa azurea
Aster frikartii Wonder of Staffa
Baptisia australis False indigo
Brunnera macrophylla
Campanula carpatica and cvs. Tussock bellflower
Campanula persicifolia Bellflower
Delphinium hybridum cvs.
Echinops ritro Globe thistle
Eryngium spp. Sea-holly
Geranium 'Johnson's Blue' Crane's-bill
Hosta ventricosa Funkia

Funkia—
a handsome foliage plant

Iris siberica (blue cvs.) Siberian iris
Iris × germanica (blue cvs.) Bearded iris
Platycodon grandiflorus and cvs. Balloon flower
Salvia × superba
Veronica spp. and cvs. Speedwell

RED/MAGENTA
Aster 'Red Star' Michaelmas daisy
Bergenia 'Evening Glow'
Centranthus ruber
Chrysanthemum cvs.
Helenium 'Moerheim Beauty'
Hemerocallis cvs. Day-lily
Iris 'Solid Mahogany'
Monarda didyma 'Adam' Bee balm
Papaver orientale cvs. Oriental poppy
Phlox paniculata 'Starfire' Summer phlox
Sedum 'Ruby Glow' Stonecrop

WHITE
Achillea ptarmica 'The Pearl' Yarrow
Agapanthus orientalis 'Albidus' African-lily
Astilbe 'Deutschland'
Bergenia 'Silver Light'
Boltonia asteroides
Chrysanthemum maximum Shasta daisy
Delphinium 'Dwarf Snow White'
Dianthus 'White Ladies'
Gypsophila paniculata 'Bristol Fairy' Baby's-breath
Helleborus niger Christmas-rose
Hosta plantaginea Plantain-lily, August-lily
Iberis sempervirens and cvs. Candytuft
Phlox paniculata 'White Admiral' Summer phlox
Physostegia virginiana 'Summer Snow' False dragonhead
Polygonatum multiflorum Solomon's seal
Verbascum chaixii 'Album' Mullein

GREEN
Alchemilla vulgaris Lady's-mantle
Euphorbia characias Spurge
Euphorbia wallichii Spurge
Galtonia viride
Helleborus corsicus Hellebore

Helleborus foetidus Hellebore
Zantedeschia aethiopica 'Green Goddess' Arum lily

Cardoon and honesty—
for decorative seedheads

PINK
Astilbe spp. and cvs.
Ajuga genevensis 'Pink Beauty' Bugleweed
Anemone × hybrida Japanese anemone, windflower
Aster spp. and cvs. Michaelmas daisy, autumn aster
Chrysanthemum morifolium cvs. Florist's garden chrysanthemum
Chrysanthemum rubellum 'Clara Curtis'
Dianthus barbatus 'Newport Pink' Sweet William
Dianthus plumarius and cvs. Cottage or grass pink
Dicentra spectabilis Bleedingheart
Hemerocallis cvs. Day-lily
Iris × germanica cvs Bearded iris
Lilium spp. and cvs. Lily
Lythrum 'Morden Pink' Loosestrife
Lycoris squamigera Magic-lily
Monarda didyma 'Croftway Pink' Bee balm
Paeonia cvs. Peony
Phlox paniculata cvs. Summer phlox
Physostegia virginiana False dragonhead
Tulipa spp. and cvs. Tulip

HANDSOME FOLIAGE PLANTS

Acaena spp. Sheepbur
Acanthus mollis and cvs. Bear's breeches
Acorus spp. Sweet flag
Ajuga spp. Bugleweed
Alchemilla vulgaris Lady's-mantle
Artemisia spp. and cvs. Wormwood
Arum italicum 'Marmoratum' Italian arum
Astrantia 'Variegata' Masterwort
Ballota nigra Black horehound
Bergenia spp. and cvs.
Brunnera macrophylla Siberian bugloss
Carex spp. Sedge
Crambe maritima Seakale
Cynara spp. Artichoke and cardoon
Daphne odora 'Variegata' Winter daphne
Epimedium spp. and cvs. Barrenwort
Eryngium spp. Sea-holly
Euonymus spp. and cvs. Spindle tree
Euphorbia spp. Spurge
Fatshedera lizei 'Variegata' Aralia-ivy
Festuca spp. and cvs. Fescue grass
Filipendula rubra 'Venusta' Meadowsweet
Glaucium phoenicium Horned poppy
Gunnera spp.
Hedera spp. and cvs. Ivy
Helleborus spp. Hellebore

White willow—
for stems in winter

Heuchera americana Alum root
Hosta spp. and cvs. Plantain-lily,
  funkia

Red oak—
for autumn interest

Houttynia cordata 'Variegata'
Iris foetidissima Gladwyn iris
Iris pallida 'Variegata' Ovris
Kerria japonica 'Aureo-variegata'
Lamium spp. and cvs. dead nettle
Ligularia spp. and cvs.
Lonicera nitida 'Baggesen's Gold'
  Honeysuckle
Lysichiton americanum Skunk-cabbage
Lysimachia nummularia 'Aurea'
  Creeping jenny
Melissa officinalis 'Aurea' Common
  balm
Mentha spp. Mint
Onopordum spp.
Origanum vulgare 'Aureum' Marjoram
Peltiphyllum peltatum Umbrella plant
Phormium tenax New Zealand flax
Physocarpus opulifolus 'Lutens'
  Ninebark
Pieris japonica 'Variegata' Variegated
  andromeda
Pulmonaria spp. Lungwort
Rheum palmatum Rhubarb
Rodgersia podophylla Rodger's bronze
  leaf
Ruta graveolens Rue
Salvia argentea Silver sage

Salvia officinalis 'Purpurascens'
  Purple sage
Salvia officinalis 'Tricolor' Sage
Saxifraga cortusifolia fortunei Saxifrage
Saxifraga × *urbium* London pride
Scrophularia nodosa 'Variegata'
  Figwort
Sedum spp. and cvs. Stonecrop
Senecio spp. and cvs. Groundsel
Sisyrinchium 'Variegatum' Blue-eyed
  grass
Stipa arundinacea Feather grass
Symphoricarpos orbiculatus 'Variegatus'
  Coralberry
Tellima grandiflora Fringecup
Thymus 'Golden Carpet' Thyme
Trifolium repens 'Purpurea' Clover
Verbascum olympicum Mullein
Veronica gentianoides 'Variegata'
  Speedwell

DECORATIVE SEEDHEADS

Acanthus spinosissimus Bear's breechies
Achillea filipendulina Yarrow
Agapanthus spp. African lily
Agrostis nebulosa Cloud grass
Allium aflatunense
Anaphalis spp. Life-everlasting
Aquilegia spp. and cvs. Columbine
Armeria spp. and cvs. Thrift
Artemisia ludoviciana Western
  mugwort

Elder—
for autumn interest

Asphodeline lutea Asphodel
Ballota spp.
Bromus spp. Bromegrass

Snowdrop—
for winter flowers

Briza spp. Quaking grass
Carex pendula Blue grass
Carlina acaulis 'Caulescens' Carline
  thistle
Celastrus spp. Bittersweet
Clematis tangutica Virgin's bower
Coix lacrima-jobi Job's-tears
Cortaderia selloana Pampas grass
Crocosmia spp. Montbretia
Cynara cardunculus Cardoon
Cyperus vegetus
Dictamnus albus and cvs. Gas plant
Dierama spp. and cvs. Wandflower
Digitalis spp. and cvs. Foxglove
Eryngium spp. Sea-holly
Filipendula spp. Meadowsweet
Galtonia candicans Summer-hyacinth
Hosta spp. and cvs. Plantain-lily
Iris chrysographes foetidissima Gladwyn
  iris
Iris innominatas
Iris sibirica Siberian iris
Lunaria annua Money plant
Lunaria rediviva Honesty
Lysimachia ephemerum Loosestrife
Miscanthus 'Zebrinus' Zebra grass
Morina longifolia Whorl flower
Nigella damascena Love-in-a-mist

Pennisetum setaceum Fountain grass
Phlomis samia
Phragmites australis Common reed

Bush bean—
a decorative vegetable

Physalis franchettii Chinese lantern
Primula florindae Primrose
Pulsatilla vulgaris Pasque flower
Rhus cotinus Sumach
Stachys byzantina Woolly betony,
 lamb's ears
Stipa spp. Feather grass
Thalictrum aquilegifolium Meadow rue
Verbascum chaixii Nettle-leaved
 mullein
Verbascum olympicum Mullein

AUTUMN INTEREST

TREES
Acer spp. and cvs. Maple
Aesculus hippocastanum Horse
 chestnut
Amelanchier spp. Shadblow
Betula spp. and cvs. Birch
Carpinus betulus Hornbeam
Cornus florida Flowering dogwood
Crataegus lavallei Lavalle hawthorn
Crataegus phaenopyrum Washington
 thorn

Fagus sylvatica Beech
Fraxinus excelsior 'Altena' Ash
Fraxinus 'Jaspidea' Ash
Fraxinus spp. and cvs. Ash
Malus coronaria and cvs. American
 crab apple
Nyssa sylvatica Sourgum
Oxydendrum arboreum Sourwood
Parrotia persica
Picea spp. and cvs. Spruce
Populus spp. and cvs. Poplar, aspen
Prunus spp. and cvs. Cherry, peach,
 plum
Quercus spp. and cvs. Oak
Sassafras albidum
Sequoia spp. Californian redwood
Sorbus aucuparia European mountain
 ash

SHRUBS
Abelia × *grandiflora* and cvs. Glossy
 abelia
Aronia arbutifolia Red chokeberry
Artemisia spp. and cvs. Wormwood
Berberis spp. and cvs. Barberry
Buddleia spp. and cvs. Butterfly bush
Callicarpa spp. and cvs. Beautyberry
Celastrus spp. Bittersweet
Cercidiphyllum japonicum Katsura tree
Clethra alnifolia Summersweet
Cornus spp. and cvs. Dogwood
Cotinus spp. and cvs. Smokebush
Cotoneaster spp. and cvs.

Wild hop—
a climbing herb

Cyrilla racemiflora Leatherwood
Deutzia spp. and cvs.
Enkianthus spp.
Euonymus spp. and cvs.
Fothergilla spp. American witch hazel
Hamamelis spp. and cvs. Witch hazel
Hebe spp.
Hedera spp. and cvs. Ivy
Hydrangea quercifolia Oakleaf
 hydrangea
Ilex spp. and cvs. Holly

Blackberries and cooking apple

Leucothoe spp. and cvs.
Lindera benzoin Spicebush
Nandina domestica Heavenly-bamboo
Osmanthus spp. and cvs.
Pachysandra spp.
Parthenocissus spp. and cvs.
 Woodbine, Virginia-creeper
Petrophytum spp. Rock-spiraea
Phlomis spp.
Pieris spp. and cvs. Andromeda
Potentilla spp. and cvs. Cinquefoil
Punica granatum and cvs.
 Pomegranate
Rhamnus spp. Buckthorn
Rhododendron spp. and cvs.
 Deciduous and evergreen azalea
Rhus spp. Sumach
Ribes spp. Currant, gooseberry
Rosa rubrifolia Rose
Rosa rugosa Rose
Sambucus spp. Elderberry
Santolina spp. Lavender cotton
Senecio spp.

Stephanandra incisa
Stranvaesia davidiana
Symphoricarpus spp. and cvs.
  Snowberry

Stonecrop—
with flowers for drying

Vaccinium spp. and cvs. Blueberry
Viburnum spp. and cvs.
Vinca spp. Periwinkle
Weigela spp. and cvs.

LATE WINTER TO EARLY SPRING FLOWER COLOR

Abeliophyllum disticum White-forsythia
Bauhinia monandra Butterfly flower
Camellis japonica and cvs.
Camellia sasanqua and cvs
Chimonanthus praecox Winter sweet
Cornus mas Cornelian-cherry
Corylopsis spp. Winter-hazel
Daphne mezereum February daphne
Eranthis spp. Winter aconite
Erica carnea and cvs. Spring heath
Euphorbia spp. Spurge
Fatsia japonica Japanese aralia
Forsythia spp. and cvs. Golden bells
Galanthus spp. Snowdrop
Garrya elliptica Silk tassel bush
Hamamelis spp. and cvs. Witch hazel
Helleborus spp. Hellebore

Jasminum nudiflorum Winter jasmine
Lindera benzoin Spicebush
Lonicera fragrantissima Honeysuckle
Magnolia stellata Star magnolia
Mahonia japonica Oregon-grape
Narcissus spp. and cvs. Daffodil, jonquil
Osmanthus fragrans Sweet-olive
Pachysandra spp.
Parrotia persica
Pieris spp. and cvs. Andromeda, fetterbush
Pulmonaria saccharata
Rhododendron spp. and cvs. Rhododendron and azalea
Sarcococca hookerana Sweet box
Skimmia japonica Japanese skimmia
Stachyurus praecox
Viburnum bodnantense
Viburnum farreri and cvs. Fragrant viburnum
Viburnum tinus Laurustinus

COLORED STEMS

Acer palmatum 'Senkaki' Maple
Arbutus spp. and cvs. Strawberry tree
Cornus alba and cvs. Tartarian dogwood
Cornus sanguinea and cvs. Blood-twig dogwood
Cornus sericea Red-osier Dogwood
Euonymus alatus Spindle tree
Euonymus phellomanus Spindle tree
Kerria japonica Japanese-rose
Leucothoe fontanesiana 'Rainbow' Drooping leucothoe
Leycesteria formosa Himalayan honeysuckle
Perovskia × 'Blue Spire'
Poncirus trifoliata Hardy orange
Ribes speciosum Fuchsia-flowered gooseberry
Salix alba chermesina White willow
Salix alba vitellina Golden willow
Salix cinera 'Variegata' Willow
Salix elaeagnos Willow
Salix fargesii Willow
Salix triandra Willow

Box—
for formal hedging

Spartium junceum Spanish broom
Stephanandra incisa 'Crispa'
Stephanandra tanakae
Ulex spp. Gorse

DECORATIVE VEGETABLES

Allium cepa Onion, Welsh and tree
Beta vulgaris Beet, Swiss chard
Brassica oleracea capitata Cabbage, red, flowering or decorative
Brassica oleracea Flowering cabbage and flowering kale
Capsicum cvs. Pepper
Cichorium endivia Endive
Crambe maritima Sea kale
Cucurbita pepo Courgettes, zucchini, golden vegetable marrow, squash
Cynara cardunculus Cardoon
Cynara scolymus Globe artichoke
Lycopersicon lycopersicum Tomato, bush cherry forms
Phaseolus vulgaris Bush bean, runner (climbing) bean
Solanum melongena esculentum Eggplant
Zea mays Sweet corn

PLANTS FOR SPECIFIC SOILS AND LOCATIONS

The following lists encompass all types of plants from field trees down to flowering annuals. You will notice that many plants have a tolerance of different soil types and locations and that your garden's overall planting list is only made truly exclusive if your conditions can be considered extreme, such as a cliff top or a bog. The lists include both American natives as well as exotic (introduced) plants, some of which have escaped from gardens and appear to be "wild."

MOIST AND SWAMPY SITES

TREES

Abies spp. Fir
Acer negundo Maple
Acer rubrum Swamp maple, red maple
Alnus spp. Alder
Amelanchier spp. June berry, shadblow
Aralia spinosa Devil's walking stick
Betula lenta Sweet birch
Betula nigra River birch, black birch
Betula papyrifera Paper birch
Calocedrus decurrens California incense-cedar
Carpinus caroliniana American hornbeam
Carya illinoinensis Pecan
Cedrus deodara Deodar
Crataegus oxyacantha and cvs. English hawthorn
Eucryphia spp. and cvs.
Fraxinus excelsior and cvs. European ash
Fraxinus nigra Black ash
Ilex decidua and cvs. Holly, possum haw
Ilex opaca American holly
Liquidambar styraciflua Sweet gum
Liriodendron tulipifera and cvs. Tulip tree
Magnolia grandiflora Bull bay, southern magnolia
Mespilus germanica Medlar
Metasequoia glyptostroboides Dawn redwood
Nothofagus antarctica Antarctic beech
Nyssa sylvatica Soler gum
Nyssa aquatica Cotton gum
Oxydendrum arboreum Sorrel tree
Parrotia persica
Picea sitchensis Sitka spruce
Populus spp. and cvs. Poplar
Prunus padus and cvs. Bird cherry
Pterocarya spp. Wing nut
Quercus bicolor Swamp white oak
Salix exigua Willow
Salix spp. and cvs. Willow
Sorbus aucuparia and cvs.
Stewartia spp. and cvs.

Taxodium distichum Bald cypress
Thuja occidentalis American arborvitae
Thuja dolarbrata False arborvitae

SHRUBS

Andromeda polifolia Bog-rosemary
Aronia arbutifolia Red chokeberry
Calluna vulgaris Heather
Calycanthus spp. Sweet shrub
Chamaedaphne calyculata Leatherleaf
Cassiope spp.
Cephalanthus occidentale Buttonbush
Clethra spp. and cvs. Summer sweet
Cornus servicea Red-osier dogwood

Calico bush—
for moist acid soils

Coronilla emerus Scorpion senna
Coronilla valentina
Cyrilla racemiflora
Dirca palustris Leatherwood
Eupatorium cannabinum Hemp-agrimony
Fothergilla spp.
Franklinia alatamaha Franklin tree
Gaultheria shallon Salal
Ilex glabra Inkberry
Ilex verticillata Winterberry
Itea virginica Virginia sweet-spire
Kalmia poliifolia Bog laurel
Leucothoe spp. and cvs. Fetterbush
Lindera benzoin Spicebush
Neillia longiracemosa Nine bark
Pernettya spp. and cvs. Prickly heath
Philadelphus spp. Mock orange

Rhamnus frangula Buckthorn
Rhododendron maximum Rosebay rhododendron
Rhododendron nudiflorum Pinxterbloom
Rhododendron vaseyi Pinkshell azalea
Rhododendron viscosum Swamp azalea
Rosa palustris Swamp rose
Salix caprea Goat willow
Sambucus spp. Elderberry
Spiraea tormentosa Hardhack
Symphoricarpos spp. and cvs. Snowberry
Viburnum lantana Wayfaring tree
Viburnum opulus Guelder rose
Vitis riparia Riverbank grape

PERENNIALS

Achillea ptarmica Sneezewort
Aconitum spp. Monk's hood
Ajuga reptans Bugleweed
Anemone hybrids Windflower
Aruncus dioicus Goat's beard
Asarum europaeum Wild evergreen ginger
Astilbe spp. and cvs. False goatsbeard
Barbarea vulgaris Common yellow rocket
Calla palustris Bog arum
Caltha palustris Marsh-marigold
Cardamine pratensis Cuckooflower
Carex morrowii and cvs. Japanese sedge grass
Chelone glabra Turtlehead
Cicuta maculata Spotted cowbane, water-hemlock
Cirsium arvense Canada thistle
Claytonia caroliniana Spring beauty
Dipsacus pilosus Small teasel
Epilobium anguslifolium Fireweed
Equisetum spp. Horsetail
Eupatorium maculatum Joe-Pye weed
Eupatorium perfoliatum Boneset
Eupatorium purpureum Joe-Pye weed
Filipendula ulmaria Meadowsweet
Galax urceolata Wandflower
Geum rivale Water avens
Glyceria maxima Reed sweet-grass
Gunnera spp. Prickly rhubarb
Helonias bullata Swamp-pink
Heloniopsis orientalis
Hemerocallis cvs. Daylily

Hibiscus mosheutos Swamp mallow
Hypericum tetrapterum Square-stalked St John's-wort
Iris foetidissima Gladwyn iris
Iris fulra Copper iris
Iris laevigata and cvs.
Iris pseudacorus Yellow flag
Iris versicolor Wild iris
Iris virginica Blue flag
Juncus effusus Soft rush
Ligularia spp. and cvs.
Lobelia cardinalis Cardinal flower
Lotus pedunculatus Marsh bird's-foot-trefoil
Luzula campestris Field wood-rush
Luzula sylvatica Greater wood-rush
Lysimachia clethroides
Lythrum salicaria Purple loosestrife
Lythrum virgatum and cvs. Loosestrife
Mentha aquatica Water mint
Menyanthes trifoliata Bog bean, marsh trefoil
Mimulus guttatus Monkey flower
Molinia caerulea Purple moor-grass
Monarda didyma and cvs. Bee balm
Myosotis scorpioides Water forget-me-not
Myosotis sylvatica and cvs. Forget-me-not
Osmunda regalis Royal fern
Peltiphyllum peltatum Umbrella plant
Petasites hybridus Butterbur
Polygonum bistorta Bistort
Pontederia cordata Pickerel weed
Primula bulleyana Primrose
Primula florindae Primrose
Primula japonica and cvs. Primrose
Primula pulverulenta Primrose
Ranunculus spp. and cvs. Buttercup
Rhexia virginica Meadow-beauty
Rodgersia spp. and cvs.
Salvia uliginosa Bog sage
Sanguisorbia canadensis American burnet
Scutellaria spp. and cvs. Skull cap
Senecio aquaticus Marsh ragwort
Senecio tanguticus Groundsel
Smilacina racemosa False Solomon's-seal
Spartina pectinata Fresh water cordgrass
Succisa pratensis Devil's-bit scabious

Symphytum officinale Comfrey
Trollius spp. and cvs. Globe flower
Typha spp. Cat-tail

English oak—
a naturalized tree

Valeriana officinalis Common
  valerian, garden-heliotrope
Vancouveria hexandra
Verbena corymbosa Vervain
Veronia spp. Ironweed
Veronica beccabunga Brooklime
Veronicastrum virginicum Culver's root
Viola palustris Marsh violet
Vitis riparia Vine

NEAR THE SEA

TREES
Acacia spp. and cvs.
Acer campestre Field maple
Acer platanoides Norway maple
Acer pseudoplatnus Sycamore
Ailanthus altissima Tree-of-heaven
Alnus glutinosa Black Alder
Araucaria heterophylla Norfolk
  Island-pine
Betula pendula Birch
Caragana arborescens Siberian pea-tree
Castanea sativa Sweet chestnut
Crataegus monogyna Hawthorn
Eucalyptas spp. and cvs. Gumtree

Fraxinus excelsior Ash
Ilex spp. Holly
Juniperus virginiana and cvs. Red-cedar
Pinus thunbergiana Japanese black pine
Populus tremula Aspen
Prunus serotina Wild black cherry
Prunus spinosa Blackthorn
Robinia pseudoacacia Black locust
Salix alba White willow
Salix cinerea Gray willow
Sorbus aria and cvs. Whitebeam
Sorbus intermedia Whitebeam

SHRUBS
Abelia × *grandiflora* Glossy abelia
Amelanchier canadensis
Arbutus unedo Strawberry tree
Arctosphylos uva-ursi Bearberry
Arundinaria spp. and cvs. Bamboo
Atriplex spp. Salt bush
Aucuba japonica Japanese laurel
Berberis (deciduous varieties) Barberry
Buddleia davidii and cvs. Butterfly bush
Ceanothus spp. and cvs. California-lilac
Choisya ternata Mexican orange
  blossom
Cistus spp. Rock-rose
Colutea arborescens Bladder senna
Corlma conradii Broom crowberry
Cornus sanguinea Dogwood
Cotoneaster (deciduous spp. and cvs.)
Elaeagnus angustifolia Russian-olive
Escallonia spp.
Euonymus japonica Spindle tree
Fuchsia cvs.
Garrya elliptica
Genista spp. Broom
Griselinia littoralis
Hebe brachysiphon
Hebe salicifolia
Hebe speciosa and cvs.
Hippophae rhamnoides Sea buckthorn
Hudsonia ericoides Beach-heather
Hypericum spp. and cvs. St John's-wort
Ilex glabra Inkberry
Ilex opaca American holly
Leiophyllum buxifolium Sand-myrtle
Myrica pensylvanica Bayberry
Olearia haastii Daisy bush
Olearia macrodonta New Zealand-holly
Pittosporum fobira Mock-orange
Pyracantha spp. and cvs. Firethorn

Ribes sanguineum Flowering currant
Rosa pimpinellifolia Scotch rose
Rosa rubiginosa Rose
Rosa rugosa Japanese rose

Blackthorn—
for coastal gardens

Rosmarinus officinalis Rosemary
Salix cinerea Gray willow
Salix viminalis Osier willow
Sambucus spp. Elderberry
Senecio spp. Groundsel
Spartium junceum Spanish broom
Tamarix spp. Tamarisk
Ulex europaeus Gorse
Viburnum lantana Wayfaring tree
Viburnum opulus Guelder rose
Viburnum tinus Laurustinus

PERENNIALS
Abronia umbellata Sand verbena
Achillea millefolium Yarrow
Agapanthus campanulatus African-lily
Alcea rosea Hollyhock
Allium cernuum Nodding onion
Allium christophii Stars of Persia
Allium senescens
Alstroemeria ligtu and cvs.
  Peruvian-lily
Althaea officinalis Marsh mallow
Anemone × *hybrida* Japanese anemone
Anthemis tinctoria Golden marguerite
Arenaria spp. and cvs. Sandwort
Armeria spp. and cvs. Thrift, sea-pink
Artemisia stelleriana Beach wormwood
Aster spp. and cvs. (low growing)
Bergenia spp.
Campanula spp. and cvs.
  (low growing) Bellflower

Sea buckthorn—
for coastal gardens

Catananche caerulea Cupid's dart
Centaurea spp. and cvs. Knapweed
Chrysanthemum spp. and cvs.
Chrysopsis mariana Golden-aster
Coreopsis lanceola Tickseed
Crambe maritima Seakale
Crocosmia spp.
Dianthus spp. and cvs. Pink
Dierama gracile Wandflower
Echinops ritro Globe thistle
Erigeron spp. Fleabane
Erodium spp. Heron's bill
Eryngium spp. Sea-holly
Euphorbia spp. (low forms) Spurge
Filipendula hexapetala Dropwort
Gaillardia aristata Blanket flower
Geranium spp. Crane's-bill
Gypsophila spp. and cvs. Baby's
   breath
Heuchera spp. and cvs. Alum-root
Iris spp. and cvs.
Kniphofia spp. and cvs. Torch lily
Liatris spp. Blazing star
Libertia formosa
Limonium spp. Sea-lavender
Linaria spp. Toadflax
Lychnis flos-jovis Flower-of-Love
Lythrum salicaria Loosestrife
Melissa offininalis Balm
Mimulus spp. Monkey flower
Morina longifolia Whorl flower
Nerine bowdenii
Oenothera spp. and cvs.
   Evening-primrose

Origanum spp.
Penstemon spp. and cvs. Beard tongue
Phormium tenax New Zealand flax
Phygelius capensis Cape-fuchsia
Physostegia virginiana False
   dragonhead
Polygonum bistorta Bistort
Potentilla spp. and cvs. Cinquefoil
Ruta spp. Rue
Salvia spp.and cvs. (low growing)
   Sage
Santolina spp. and cvs. Lavender
   cotton
Scabiosa spp. Scabious
Schizostylis coccinea Kaffir-lily
Scrophularia aquatica Water figwort
Sedum spp. Stonecrop
Sisyrinchium spp. Satin flower
Solidago spp. Goldenrod
Stachys spp. Woundwort
Stokesia laevis Stoke's aster
Thymus spp. and cvs. Thyme
Tritonia rubrolucens
Veronica spp. and cvs. Speedwell
Yucca filimentosa Adam's needle

VINES AND CREEPERS
Arctostaphylos uva-ursi Bearberry
Celastris scandens Bittersweet
Juniperus conferta Shore juniper
Juniperus horizontalis and cvs. Creeping
   juniper
Lathrys latifolius Perennial pea
Lonicera japonica halliana Hall's
   honeysuckle
Parthenocissus quinquefolia Virginia-
   creeper

Thrift—
a seaside perennial

GRAVEL

TREES
Acer negundo Box elder
Acer platanoides Norway maple
Acer pseudoplatanus Sycamore-maple
Aesculus spp. Horse chestnut
Ailanthus altissima Tree-of-heaven
Albizia julibrissin Silk tree
Amelanchier spp. Shadblow
Betula pendula European white birch
Betula populifolia gray birch
Caragana spp. Pea tree
Carpinus spp. Hornbeam
Celtis spp. Hackberry
Crataegus spp. and cvs. Hawthorn
Fagus spp. and cvs. Beech
Morus alba White mulberry
Platanus spp. Plane tree, sycamore
Pinus nigra Austrian pine
Populus spp. Poplar
Prunus avium Sweet cherry
Prunus pensylvanicica Wild red cherry
Prunus virginiana Chokeberry
Quercus spp. and cvs. Oak
Salix spp. Willow
Sassafras albidum
Sorbus spp. Whitebeam, mountain-ash
Tilia spp. and cvs. Lime, linden

SHRUBS
Amelanchier spp. Shadbush
Artemisia arborescens Shrubby
   wormwood
Berberis spp. and cvs. Barberry
Cistus spp. and cvs. Rock rose
Clerodendrum spp. and cvs.
   Glory-bower
Cortaderia selloana Pampas grass
Corylus spp. and cvs. Filbert, hazlenut
Cotoneaster spp. and cvs.
Cytisus spp. and cvs. Broom
Elaeagnus spp. and cvs.
Elsholtzia stauntonii Mint shrub
Genista spp. Broom
Helianthemum nummularium Sun rose
Hippophae rhamnoides Sea buckthorn
Hypericum spp. St John's-wort
Juniperus spp. and cvs. Juniper
Mahonia aquifolium Oregon grape
Mahonia repens Creeping mahonia

Plane tree—
for planting through gravel

Phlomis fruticosa Jerusalem-sage
Potentilla spp. and cvs. Cinquefoil
Rhus spp. and cvs. Sumach
Romneya coulteri Californian
   tree-poppy
Rosmarinus officinalis Rosemary
Spartium junceum Spanish broom
Spiraea spp. and cvs.
Stephanandra incisa
Symphoricarpus spp. and cvs.
   Snowberry
Tamarix spp. Tamarisk
Ulex spp. Gorse

WOODLAND

TREES
Acer circinatum Vine maple
Acer griseum Paperbark maple
Acer palmatum and cvs. Japanese
   maple
Acer pseudoplatinus Sycamore maple
Acer pensylvanicum Moosewood
Alnus crispa American alder
Amelanchier spp. and cvs. Shadblow
Betula spp. and cvs. Birch
Carpinus caroliniana American
   hornbeam
Carys spp. Hickory
Cercis canadensis Eastern redbud
Cornus florida Flowering dogwood
Cornus kousa chinensis Chinese
   dogwood

Cornus nuttallii Mountain dogwood
Corylus spp. Hazlenut
Crataegus spp. and cvs. Hawthorn
Fagus spp. and cvs. Beech
Fraxinus spp. and cvs. Ash
Halesia spp. Silver bell tree
Ilex spp. and cvs. Holly
Laris decidua Larch
Lindera benzoin Spicebush
Oxydendrum arboreum Sourwood
Parrotia persica
Photinia villosa
Nyssa sylvatica Sour gum
Picea spp. and cvs. Spruce
Pinus spp. and cvs. Pine
Quercus spp. and cvs. Oak
Rhododendron maximum Rosebay
Sassafras akbidum
Taxus spp. and cvs. Yew
Tsuga spp. and cvs. Hemlock

Beech—
a woodland tree

SHRUBS
Aucuba japonica and cvs. Japanese
   aucuba
Camellia spp. and cvs.
Chionanthus virginicus Fringe tree
Clethra spp. and cvs. Summersweet
Cornus mas Cornelian-cherry
Corylopsis spp. and cvs. Winter hazel
Daphne spp. and cvs.
Enkianthus spp. and cvs.
Fothergilla spp.

Gaultheria shallon Salal
Hamamelis spp. and cvs. Witch hazel
Hydrangea quercifolia Oakleaf
   hydrangea
Ilex spp. and cvs. Holly
Itea virginica Virginia sweetspire
Kalmia latifolia Mountain-laurel
Laurus nobilis Sweet bay
Leucothoe spp. and cvs. Drooping
   leucothoe
Nandina domestica Heavenly-bamboo
Osmanthus spp. and cvs.
Pieris floribunda American andromeda
Pieris japonica and cvs. Japanese
   andromeda
Pittosporum tobira and cvs. Japanese
   pittosporum, mock-orange
Prunus laurocerasus Cherry-laurel
Rhododendron spp. and cvs.
Skimmia spp
Taxus spp. and cvs. yew
Vaccinium spp. and cvs. Blueberry
Viburnum acerifolium Maple-leaved
   viburnum
Viburnum dentatum Arrow-wood
Viburnum opulus Guelder-rose
Viburnum prunifolium Black haw

WILDFLOWERS
Actea spp. Baneberry, cohosh
Anemonella thalictroides Rue anemone
Aquilegia caerulea Rocky Mt.
   columbine

Wild strawberry—
a woodland perennial

Aquilegia canadensis Wild columbine
Asarum canadense Wild-ginger, snakeroot
Caulophyllum thalictroides Blue cohosh
Chelone glabra Turtlehead, snakehead
Chimaphila spp. Spotted wintergreen, pipsissewa
Chiogenes hispidula Creeping snowberry
Clintonia spp. Bead-lily
Cornus canadensis Bunchberry
Cypripedium spp. Lady-slipper
Dicentra cucullaria Dutchman's-breeches
Dicentra eximia Wild bleedingheart, turkey corn
Dicentra formosa Western bleedingheart
Dodecatheon spp. Shooting-star
Epigaea repens Trailing-arbutus
Galax urceolata Wandflower
Gaultheria procumbens Wintergreen
Geranium maculatum Wild-geranium
Goodyera spp. Rattlesnake-plantain
Hepatica acutiloba Liverleaf
Hepatica americana Liverleaf
Jeffersonia diphylla Twinleaf
Linnaea borealis Twinflower
Maianthemum canadense Wild lily-of-the-valley
Mertensia virginica Virginia bluebells
Mitchella repens Partridge-berry
Mitella diphylla Bishop's-cap
Monotropa uniflora Indian pipe
Phlox divaricata Wild blue phlox
Phlox stolonifera Creeping phlox
Podophyllum peltatum May-apple
Polemonium reptams Jacob's-ladder
Polygala paucifolia fringed milkwort, gay-wings
Polygonatum commutatum Great Solomon's-seal
Sanguinaria canadense Bloodroot
Shortia galacifolia Oconee-bells
Smilacina racemosa False Solomon's-seal
Streptopus roseus Twisted stalk
Tiarella cordifolia Foamflower
Trientalis borealis American starflower
Triullium spp. Wake-robin
Uvularia spp. Merrybells, bellwort

Maidenhair tree—
for chalky soil

Vaccinium vitis-idaea var. *minus* Cowberry
Vancouveria hexandra
Viola spp. Violet

CHALKY SOIL

TREES

Abies grandis Giant fir
Abies koreana Korean fir
Acer campestre Field maple
Acer cappadocicum and cvs. Vine maple
Acer griseum Paperbark maple
Acer negundo and cvs. Box elder
Acer platanoides and cvs. Norway maple
Acer pseudoplatanus and cvs. Sycamore maple
Acer saccharum and cvs. Sugar maple
Aesculus hippocastanum Horse chestnut
Ailanthus altissima Tree-of-heaven
Amelanchier spp. Shadblow
Betula spp. and cvs. Birch
Caragana arborescens Siberian pea tree
Carpinus betulus Hornbeam
Cedrus spp. and cvs. Cedar
Corylus avellana Cobnut
Cotoneaster spp. and cvs.
Crataegus monogyna English hawthorn
Davidia involucrata Dove tree
Fagus spp. and cvs. Beech
Fraxinus excelsior and cvs. European ash
Fraxinus ornus and cvs. Flowering ash
Fraxinus oxycarpa Ash

Fraxinus relutina Arizona ash
Ginkgo biloba Maidenhair tree
Gleditsia triacanthos and cvs. Honey locust
Juglans spp. Walnut
Juniperus × media and cvs. Juniper
Juniperus × media 'Plumosa aurea' Juniper
Juniperus squamata and cvs. Juniper
Juniperus virginiana 'Grey Owl' Juniper
Koelreuteria paniculata Golden-rain tree
Laburnum spp. Golden-chain tree
Liriodendron tulipera Tulip tree
Magnolia kobus
Malus spp. Crab apple
Morus spp. Mulberry
Paulownia tomentosa Princess tree
Populus spp. Poplar
Prunus spp. and cvs. Cherry, plum, peach
Pyrus spp. and cvs. Pear
Quercus cerris Turkey oak
Quercus robur English oak
Robinia pseudoacacia False acacia
Sophora japonica Pagoda tree
Sorbus aria and cvs. Whitebeam
Sorbus hybrida
Sorbus intermedia Swedish whitebeam
Tilia spp. and cvs. Lime, linden

SHRUBS

Aesculus parviflora Dwarf buckeye
Arundinaria spp. Bamboo
Aucuba japonica and cvs. Japanese-laurel
Berberis spp. and cvs. (deciduous and evergreen) Barberry
Buddleia spp. and cvs. Butterfly bush
Ceanothus spp. and cvs.
Choisya ternata Mexican orange blossom
Cistus spp. and cvs. Rock-rose
Clerodendrum trichotomum Glory bower
Colutea arborescens Bladder senna
Cornus mas Cornelian-cherry
Cotoneaster spp. and cvs.
Cytisus nigricans Broom
Daphne mezereum February daphne
Deutzia spp. and cvs.

Elaeagnus spp. and cvs.
Escallonia spp. and cvs.
Eucryphia spp. and cvs.
Euonymus spp. and cvs.
Forsythia spp. and cvs. Golden bells
Fuchsia spp. and cvs.
Hedera spp. and cvs. Ivy
Hydrangea macrophylla
Hydrangea villosa
Hypericum spp. and cvs. St John's-wort
Ilex spp. and cvs. Holly
Indigofera spp. Indigo
Kerria japonica and cvs. Japanese-rose
Kolkwitzia amabilis Beauty bush
Mahonia aquifolium and cvs. Oregon grape
Olearia spp. Daisy bush
Osmanthus spp. and cvs.
Paeonia spp. and cvs. Peony
Philadelphus spp. Mock orange
Phlomis spp.
Pittosporum spp. and cvs. Mock-orange
Potentilla spp. and cvs. Cinquefoil
Prunus laurocerasus and cvs. Cherry-laurel
Pyracantha spp. and cvs. Firethorn
Rhus spp. Sumach
Ribes spp.
Romneya coulteri Californian tree-poppy
Rosmarinus spp. and cvs. Rosemary
Rubus spp. and cvs. Blackberry
Sambucus spp. Elderberry
Santolina spp. Lavender cotton
Sarcococca hookerana Sweet box

Brewer's weeping spruce—
for clay soil

Senecio spp. Groundsel
Spartium junceum Spanish broom
Spiraea spp. and cvs.
Staphylea spp. Bladder nut
Symphoricarpus spp. and cvs. Snowberry
Syringa spp. and cvs. Lilac
Tamarix spp. Tamarisk
Teucrium chamaedrys Germander
Ulex spp. Gorse
Viburnum spp. and cvs.
Vinca spp. Periwinkle
Weigela florida and cvs.

CLAY SOIL

TREES
Abies spp. Fir
Acer campestre Maple
Aesculus hippocastanum Horse chestnut
Alnus spp. and cvs. Alder
Betula pendula European white birch
Carpinus betulus Hornbeam
Cornus spp. and cvs. Dogwood
Corylus avellana Cobnut
Crataegus spp. and cvs. Hawthorn
Fraxinus spp. and cvs. Ash
Malus spp. and cvs. Apple and crab apple
Picea brewerana Spruce
Platanus orientalis Plane tree
Populus spp. and cvs. Poplar
Prunus spp. and cvs. Plum, cherry, peach
Pyrus spp. and cvs. Peare
Quercus spp. and cvs. Oak
Salix spp. and cvs. Willow
Sorbus aria White beam
Taxus baccata and cvs. English yew
Thuja plicata and cvs. Western red cedar
Tilia spp. and cvs. Lime, linden

SHRUBS
Aesculus hippocastanum Horse chestnut
Aralia spp.
Aucuba japonica and cvs. Japanese laurel

Flowering quince—
for clay soil

Berberis spp. and cvs. Barberry
Chaenomeles spp.and cvs. Flowering quince
Choisya ternata Mexican orange blossom
Cornus spp.and cvs. Dogwood
Corylus avellana Cobnut
Cotoneaster spp. and cvs.
Euonymus spp. and cvs.
Forsythia spp. and cvs. Golden bells
Hedera spp. and cvs. Ivy
Hypericum spp.and cvs. St John's-wort
Kerria japonica Japanese-rose
Osmanthus spp. and cvs. False holly
Philadelphus spp. and cvs. Mock orange
Potentilla spp. and cvs. Cinquefoil
Prunus laurocerasus and cvs. Cherry laurel
Pyracantha spp. and cvs. Firethorn
Rhamnus frangula Buckthorn
Ribes spp. and cvs. Currant, gooseberry
Rosa spp. and cvs. Rose
Rubus spp. and cvs. Blackberry
Salix spp. and cvs. Willow
Skimmia japonica Japanese skimmia
Spiraea spp. and cvs.
Symphoricarpos spp. and cvs. Snowberry
Syringa spp. and cvs. Lilac
Viburnum spp. and cvs.
Vinca spp. Periwinkle
Weigela spp. and cvs.

Daylily—
for clay soil

PERENNIALS

Acanthus balcanicus Bear's breeches
Acanthus mollis Artist's acanthus
Alchemilla spp. Lady's mantle
Anemone × *hybrida* Windflower
Aruncus sylvester Goat's beard
Bergenia spp.
Brunnera macrophylla Siberian bugloss
Caltha palustris Marsh-marigold
Epimedium spp. and cvs. Barrenwort
Euphorbia epilhymoides Spurge
Geranium spp. and cvs. Crane's-bill
Helleborus spp. and cvs. Hellebore
Hemerocallis spp. and cvs. Daylily
Hosta spp. and cvs. Plantain-lily,
    funkia
Lamiastrum galeobdolon Yellow
    archangel
Lamium maculatum Spotted lamium

Juniper—
for sandy soil

Peltiphyllum peltatum Umbrella plant
Petasites japonicus Butterbur
Polygonatum × *hybridum* Solomon's
    seal
Primula spp. and cvs. Primrose
Prunella spp. and cvs. Selfheal
Rheum palmatum Rhubarb
Saxifraga × *urbium* Saxifrage, London
    pride
Symphytum grandiflorum Comfrey
Waldsteinia ternata

LIGHT SANDY SOIL

TREES

Acer spp. and cvs. Maples
Ailanthus altissima Tree-of-Heaven
Albizia julibrissin Silk-tree
Alnus cordata Italian alder
Arabia elata Japanese angelica
Betula populifolia Gray birch
Carya glabra Pignut
Castanea hippocastanum Chestnut
Cedrus spp. Cedar
Cercidiphyllum japonicum
Cladrastis lutea Yellow-wood
Elaeagnus angustifolia Russian-olive
Fraxinus ornus Flowering ash
Gleditsia triacanthos Honey locust
Juniperus spp. and cvs. Juniper
Maclura pomifera Osage-orange
Pinus rigida Pitch pine
Pinus sylvestris Scots pine
Pinus thunbergiana Japanese black pine
Populus alba and cvs. White poplar
Querous ilicifolia Scrub oak
Quercus undula Rocky Mt. scrub oak
Robinia pseudoacacia False acacia
Salix pentandra Laurel willow
Sassafras albidum Violet willow
Ulmus parvifolia Chinese elm
Zelkova serrata Japanese zelkova

SHRUBS

Amelanchier spp. and cvs. Shadblow
Arctostaphylos uva-ursi Bearberry
Berberis spp. and cvs. Barberry
Buddleia alternafolia Fountain buddleia
Callistemon lanceolatus Lemon
    bottle-brush

Cistus spp. and cvs. Rock rose
Clerodendrum trichotomum
Colutea arborescens Bladder-senna
Comptonia perigrina Sweet-fern
Corema conradii Broom-crowberry
Cytisus spp. and cvs. Broom
Elaeagnus spp. and cvs.
Gaylussacia spp. Huckleberry
Genista spp. Broom
Hibiscus syriacus Rose-of-sharon
Hippophae rhamnoides Sea buckthorn
Hudsonia ericoides Beach-heather
Hypericum spp. and cvs. St John's-wort
Indigofera spp. Indigo
Lavandula spp. and cvs. Lavender
Lespedeza spp. Bush clover
Myrica pensylvanica Bayberry
Myrtus communis Myrtle

Sycamore maple—
for badly-drained soil

Perovskia atriplicifolia
Phlomis fruticosa Jerusalem-sage
Potentilla spp. Cinquefoil
Prunus maritima Beach plum
Prunus pumila Sand cherry
Rhus spp. Sumach
Romneya coulteri Californian
    tree-poppy
Rosa rugosa Japanese rose
Rosmarinus officinalis Rosemary
Sambucus spp. Elderberry
Shepherdia canadensis Buffalo-berry
Spartium junceum Spanish broom
Spiraea latifolia Meadowsweet
Stephanandra incisa Lace shrub
Tamarix spp. and cvs. Tamarisk
Vaccinium pallidum Dryland blueberry
Vitex agnus-castus Chaste-tree
Yucca spp. and cvs

INDEX

Page numbers in *italic* refer to illustrations and captions

ACKNOWLEDGMENTS

Author's acknowledgments
Without the help of Dorling Kindersley's in-house staff I could not have put this book together—for we have mutually beaten out the mores of the country mood through stimulating discussion and argument. I would like to thank, in particular, Meryl Lloyd and David Lamb, both of whom I have enjoyed working with immensely. Jacqui Hurst's photography was a joy with which to work as well. I had invaluable assistance from my friend Sarah Broley in Washington DC, from Jane Pooley and of course, at home base, the efficient and relentless support of my secretary Jenny Paterson.

Photographer's acknowledgments
Jacqui Hurst would like to thank everybody who allowed her to photograph their gardens for this book: Janet Allen, Major and The Hon Mrs Arbuthnot, Elsie and Henry Ball, Ellis and Henry Bull, Tom Bartlett, Anne Belam, Bob and Penny Black, Alix Blomer, Mr and Mrs Blomer, Humphrey Brooke, John and Sheila Bruce, Mr and Mrs A J Buchanan, Anthony and Elizabeth Bullivant, Beth Chatto, His Honor Judge Clay and Mrs Clay, Mr and Mrs G Clay, Mr and Mrs G Goode-Adams, Dr and Mrs J Cox, Sylvia and Colin Dales, Ann Dewar, Lord and Lady Dickinson, Dale and Alice Fishburn, Mr D Flower, Gainsborough House Trust, Mr and Mrs I Garnett-Orme, Sir Julian Gascoigne, Mr and The Hon Mrs Peter Healing, Patrick Heron, Major and Mrs A Hibbert, Penelope Hobhouse, Judith and Simon Hopkinson, Mr and Mrs W Howes-Bassett, Barrie Hurst, Hazel Hurst, Mr and Mrs J Knight, Mr and Mrs R Marshall, Mr and Mrs R Merton, Joy Moss, Mr and Mrs Norton, Mr and Mrs Palmer, Mr and Mrs A E Pedder, Mr and Mrs F Plumb, Mrs Pumphrey, Major D and Lady Anne Rasch, Mr and Mrs C A Richardson, Martyn Rix, Rodney and Pamela Russell, Mrs Sedgwick, The Hon Mrs Smith-Ryland, Mrs Sybil Spencer, Dr and Mrs Stanton, John Tann, Mrs V. Thomas, Mr and Mrs J Thompson, Myles Thoroton-Hildyard, Mrs D Verey, Mrs C L Ward, Michael and Denny Wickham, Mr and Mrs David Williams, Mr and Mrs Wright; also special thanks to David Robertson.

Dorling Kindersley would like to thank:
The Royal Botanic Gardens, Kew, Hyams and Cockerton Ltd., John Tann, Martyn Rix, Richard Bird, Simon Adams, Arthur Brown, Tessa Richardson-Jones, Kate Grant and Jenny Engelmann.

Illustrations by Vanessa Luff, Eric Thomas, Vana Haggerty, David Ashby, Peter Morter, Rodney Shackell, Imperial Artists.